DATE			

THE BOOK OF SEAMANSHIP

THE BOOK OF SEAMANSHIP

JOHN RUSSELL

ZIFF-DAVIS PUBLISHING COMPANY
New York

First U.S. Edition by
Ziff-Davis Publishing Company
One Park Avenue
New York, N.Y. 10016

ISBN 0–87165–055–X
Library of Congress Catalog Card Number 79–90879

Printed in Great Britain

Contents

List of Illustrations

DIAGRAMS

1
Set and Drift

1

The word seamanship is capable of various interpretations, ranging from the narrow sense which distinguishes the manual skills of handling ropes and all the other devices involved in the operation and maintenance of a vessel at sea and in harbour, to the whole spectrum of knowledge and ability that the seafarer must use in the management of ship and crew. I would define it as the ability to achieve one's objective on the sea.

Scores of books have been written both about the basic skills of the seaman and the many specialised subjects which concern him and, as in the course of time we harvest the fruits of discovery and develop the potential of new knowledge, scores more are written to take account of progress and bring explanation, comment and instruction up to date. To the suggestion that I should add to this extensive literature, my first reaction was to ask why. Why, when we already have the wisdom of Worth, the wide experience and meticulous thoroughness of Hiscock, to name only two of the distinguished authors who have dealt with the subject, should I imagine that anything I could add would be useful? I thought about all the technical progress that is being made in this era, but that needs a more technical mind than mine to do it justice. The guts of an electronic log looks for all the world like a very small reproduction of a carved wall panel from the temple at Karnak, its enciphered secrets inaccessible to mere mechanical aptitude. But how much do we need to know about these things? The paradox of modern technology is that it often requires less understanding to use it than to do without it. Then I remembered the words of the petty officer in charge of a party of recruits who were being shown round HMS *Victory*. 'Mind you,' he said, 'the Navy's changed since Nelson's day. The 'ammick 'ooks is two and a half inches further apart.' I was reminded how easy it is to measure progress by a material yardstick and leave it at that.

Notwithstanding the spectacular achievements of technical innovation, the most significant change to have affected yachting during the past half century has occurred in the way we live. Fifty years ago when families were more settled and lived longer in the same place, when travel was more laborious and weekends started at midday on Saturdays, most people engaged in the sports and pastimes among which they happened to live. With a few exceptions, those who took up sailing had grown up with it and had unconsciously absorbed a tremendous amount of nautical lore with the air they breathed. As children they were surrounded by fishermen and pilots, boatbuilders and sailmakers; boats were simply adjuncts to normal life, whose care and handling were learnt as a matter of course. Half their acquaintances habitually marked the passage of time by referring to natural events. Where the landsman might say, 'See you after tea', the seaman would say, 'Come around about high water', and everyone knew towards which point of the compass he was facing and kept one eye cocked for the tell-tale weather signs in the sky. The result of all this was a gradual impregnation with sea sense as a herring is impregnated with oak smoke. The seaside child old enough to walk sat down in a boat and kept his hands off the gunwales, and later his body learnt, without any scientific explanation being given to him, how the boat's fore-and-aft trim affected her lateral and directional stability, and he moved in the instinctive exercise of this knowledge just as his inland cousin did on his pony.

The rise in living standards which occurred during the middle of this century, coupled with increased personal mobility and the growth of subsidised leisure opportunities for young people have spread the growth of all kinds of watersport throughout the community, regardless of background influences. This has been accompanied by the organisation of sailing instruction in schools, the development of training and cadet sections in clubs, the opening of numerous sailing schools and the establishment of nationally recognised qualifications in several European countries. The leisurely, almost casual indoctrination by long exposure has all but disappeared and has been replaced by a more efficient, more organised and more rapid process. Nowadays the way to learn about seamanship is to start with a formal course whose aim is to teach the basic technique of sailing without refinement in a simple boat and sheltered water; then to get out in charge of a boat and consolidate the lesson with experience before going on to further instruction in more advanced or applied sailing, together with the associated disciplines of navigation, meteorology and so on through a logically progressing series. Even for those children—now a minute proportion of the huge total of amateur sailors—lucky enough to grow up by the sea, this is the best way because the environment itself has changed and those rich contacts that nourished former generations no longer exist. Boats are built behind the blank walls of factories, not on the almost open shore; their fittings, no longer forged at the roadside, come polythene wrapped from goodness knows where, and the fishermen, the pilots, the boatbuilders and sailmakers no longer stroll back to their cottages with time for a chat but leap into cars and go tearing away as if the devil were at their heels, oppressed like all of us by the time that material progress has enabled us to save.

Alongside these changes has arisen an increasing pre-occupation with the material, a tendency to concentrate upon equipment and gadgets and the methods of using them rather than upon the human element which these things are supposed to serve. Authors of books on seamanship perhaps unconsciously reinforce this tendency by dividing the subject along material lines and using chapter headings such as 'Rig', 'Ground Tackle' and so on, and this is after all a logical way for practical men to handle a practical subject which is notoriously difficult to organise in any other way. Nor can one blame the official bodies, who discharge the difficult task of ensuring that our seafaring ambitions cause the least possible waste and trouble to others by issuing lists of items that we must take with us, for what else short of total regulation can they do? But the upshot has been that almost any discussion on safety, for instance, turns out to be not about forethought and priorities but about equipment, and

moreover equipment whose purpose is not to ensure safety but to retrieve the situation when safety has been lost. It was deplorably sloppy thinking that stuck the label 'Safety Equipment' on to such things as liferafts, fire extinguishers and distress flares. These things are emergency, or if you prefer it, danger or survival equipment. Examples of true safety equipment are the humble electric fuse, the lifeline and harness, the white flare and, foremost of all, the pound or two of slush that every one of us carries around for life in his skull.

Claud Worth, writing about the Pentland Firth, surely one of the world's most formidable stretches of water, said:

> Under favourable conditions and with proper management there is nothing to fear, even in the smallest yacht.

As usual he went unerringly to the kernel of the problem: favourable conditions and proper management. If he had been writing today it is inconceivable that he would have said, 'with a reliable diesel and two-way radio' but what would our priorities have been? These words of Worth's have provided the inspiration for this book, for wherein lies the art of the seaman if not in the recognition and exploitation of favourable conditions and the exercise of proper management? My aim is not a new manual or textbook but rather a commentary that will help the amateur to make good use of existing books and of the admirable direct instruction that is now so widely available.

The first part of the book deals with the stage setting, the arena of natural forces in which the action takes place and where conditions so critically affect us. The second concerns the actors, ourselves, where management finds its most vital expression. The final section contains aspects of the action that I have chosen for a variety of reasons; because I hope to add to existing ideas; because a familiar scene is often made clearer when viewed from an unfamiliar angle; or as in the case of the chapter on seamanship in harbour, because the subject is neglected, starved of opportunities for practice and critical observation through the spread of marina basing, and squeezed into the background on formal courses by the chronic shortage of time, so that low standards are everywhere prevalent and the rare good example goes unrecognised. Throughout I have addressed myself particularly to the reader who does not readily think in scientific or mathematical terms and is often poorly served by teachers who do. This may have resulted in some approximations and half-truths as the price of intelligibility, but I can promise that no mathematical formula will appear unless it can be put to use by the reader.

As a hedonistic and unscholarly reader I have to confess to being as ignorant of the provenance of most of the ideas in my head as I am of the change in my pocket. By rights there should be a page or two of acknowledgements to all the authors from Homer onwards who have contributed to my nautical education and lifelong enjoyment, so with apologies to the rest I shall name only the two whose works wrought fundamental changes in my attitudes. To Ann Davison, for awakening me to the importance of correct priorities with her frank and courageous account of mismanagement and tragedy in *Last Voyage* (happily not her last because she subsequently became the first woman to sail alone across the Atlantic), and to Errol Bruce, whose *Deep Sea Sailing* made me realise what a lousy skipper I was and stung me into a continuing fascination with the art of captaincy, I tender heartfelt thanks.

We begin now with a story, for whose historical probability I make no claim, in which I shall try to present seamanship in terms of its essential elements of men and the sea, with all the material factors reduced to their most primitive form.

2
Point of Departure

2

Picture the first attempts at seafaring by a small group of our ancestors. Living beside the placid lower reaches of a river, they have adapted the local building materials to fashion simple log rafts which they propel and guide by quanting with staves wherever the water is deep enough to float them and shallow enough for their poles to reach the bottom. These rafts increased their freedom of movement and extended the range of their fishing, hunting and reed gathering, but as long as they were propelled by poles they merely had the effect of giving the inhabitants longer legs so that they could wade in deeper water and stronger backs to carry heavier loads: they introduced no new dimension into travel and transport, and people were still tied to the ground of the river bed just as they had been tied to the ground of the fields and forests. It is true they could swim but swimming was slow and tiring, and a swimmer could carry next to nothing. When the raft crews found themselves, as they inevitably did from time to time, in water too deep for quanting, necessity taught them how to paddle with the poles. The more thoughtful began to choose those spars that could be most effectively used as paddles, improved their shape until they came to resemble long paddles which could also be used as quants and eventually, deciding that paddling was a better method of propulsion and control, produced short handy paddles that were less tiring to use and allowed more men to work at one time. With this simple development they freed themselves from the need to maintain contact with the ground. Water, which had for so long been a barrier, now became a path. Navigation became possible.

The tribesmen explored the river. Wherever the surface of the water led they followed it. They crossed to the opposite bank. They toiled inland against the current, grounding on shoals, leaping out and dragging their craft to the next pool until the swiftness of the stream finally brought them to a halt. They idled downstream until the pulse of the tide reversed the current, alternately flooding and laying bare the banks where huge flocks of birds patrolled and foraged among the unseen creatures of the sea. They gazed out to the horizon and beheld what they had so often seen from the hill behind the village, the Island. They called it Yonderland or simply Yon. It lay on the horizon and like the hills inland it was sometimes grey and smudged, sometimes blue and clear cut, and at other times invisible, concealed in mist and cloud. Up to the time of the invention of the paddle it had merely been another part of their surroundings and had been taken for granted. It was true that some of the old men were in the habit of eyeing it sagely and making prognostications about the weather or the prospects for the harvest, and even the oldest inhabitant couldn't remember a time when someone hadn't said that if you could see Yon it was going to rain and that if you couldn't see it it was raining. But now all that was changed. Now that the sea had become a pathway Yon was a magnet that drew the thoughts of everyone with any conceivable kind of ambition whether for personal prestige, material gain, political advantage, missionary zeal, scientific curiosity, the desire to impress a girl or to escape a creditor. There was a great deal of talk and a certain amount of action. One or two raft crews simply struck out for the island as soon as they saw it, but most returned exhausted within a couple of hours, declaring that there were evil spirits in the ocean and that the voyage was impossible.

One young man, whom the villagers called Scratch because of his habit of drawing lines and shapes on the ground, decided that a voyage to Yon was possible and worthy of attempt. He began making serious unhurried preparations, saying little but listening to all whose experience seemed relevant. He began by climbing a hill at the coast and carefully comparing the appearance of Yon with the familiar local landscape in order to estimate its distance. This he decided was half-a-day's march, which could be covered by a good raft crew in about half as long again. Those who had ventured out on the ocean had reported that because of the waves paddling was much heavier work than in the river, so he would need a strong crew and a fast raft and the crew would need to be able to restore their strength with water, food and rest.

All the rafts that had so far gone to sea had had trouble with the lashings that held them together: these had stretched and in some cases failed so that the rafts had broken apart. Scratch made up his mind to develop a raft more suited to his purpose than any yet existing on the river and to use the building of this raft as the first step in forming his crew, whose members he would choose from the handful of young men who were already used to rafting with him on the river. He soon discovered how to shorten the individual turns of the lashings so that they were less liable to stretch and by a happy chance hit on the device of using wedges to keep them tight.

While his hands were thus agreeably occupied his mind considered his crew. They were all good raftmen, and to him that meant that their movements were precise and co-ordinated, with the assured delicacy of cats. A man who was clumsy on the water seemed to him to be out of his proper element, a misfit who had no place there and one to be discouraged for his own good. But it would take more than just good raftmen to make this voyage; the crew would have to be adaptable, resourceful and determined. Skills would be needed too, not just the skill in paddling that would be required of every man as a matter of course, but in the maintenance and repair of the raft, skill at sensing direction, interpreting the signs of weather and the behaviour of wild creatures, and maybe even at fighting as well.

The design of rafts was governed by the simple fact that it required two logs to support each man in the crew. Experience on the river had shown that long narrow rafts were fastest; they could employ more paddlers for a given weight of raft, but length brought the penalty of weakness, and narrowness made the rafts unstable. Scratch decided that the raft would be limited to a single log in length, for the sake of rigidity, and to six in width. The traditional way of arranging the logs had been in two layers at right angles, but using his improved bindings, he intended to have three layers all parallel, two each of six logs sandwiching a layer of five in the middle, which would give a total of seventeen logs and therefore a carrying capacity of eight paddlers.

They built the raft beside a secluded backwater, choosing the logs carefully and taking great pains over the lashings, but when launched it proved a disappointment, being heavy to paddle despite its narrow beam and tending to lurch ponderously in roll. Scratch noticed that it floated higher than the traditional two-tier rafts and thought that the three-tier arrangement might provide enough buoyancy with only fifteen logs. He accordingly removed the two outermost logs of the bottom layer. This improved the stability and made the raft easier to paddle, and while the freeboard was somewhat reduced the crew felt much happier and more confident with the feel of it under them.

Sensing the demand which the projected voyage would make on their strength and endurance, the raftmen considered how best to take advantage of natural conditions. On the river the wind had little effect on the heavy rafts but currents were crucial and everyone agreed that a strong contrary current could render Yon as inaccessible as ever. So they studied the sea for signs of currents. They had noticed that the estuary and coastal waters were unlike the river, where the current varied in strength but ran always in the same direction. The sea water advanced toward the land and retreated again twice each day, reaching its highest and lowest points a little later at each succeeding cycle, in just the same way that the moon reached the same point in the sky a little later each night. There were those who argued that, since the tide always rose as the moon moved across the sky to a certain point and fell as it moved on beyond it, either the moon must influence the tides or the tide the moon. Supporters of both propositions debated hotly but were equally unable to dispose of the objection that the tide continued to rise and fall whether the moon was there or not. Respectable people were outraged. Was not the sun Lord of all Creation? Did not the highest and lowest of all tides occur at the season of the Sacred Equinox? The women said, 'Oh you men. Would the moon husk the barley or the tide mend the children's clothes?' But to Scratch and his crew both the current that ran out of the river and away from the land on the ebb and the returning flood were favourable at different stages of their voyage, and they made up their minds that they would start at a time when high water coincided with the first light of dawn. The final stages of preparation were made close to the river mouth. Spare lengths of lashing were prepared from creeper ropes, water skins sewn and hunting rations collected. Scratch took careful note of the direction of the island and identified an alignment of marks on the mainland that he could use to get his direction if cloud should obscure the objective. He and his crew exercised daily at paddling the new raft in the tidal water of the estuary, and all the time he watched the weather for signs of a settled spell.

All these preparations were made secretly at some distance from the village because the tribal council had decided that it could enhance its prestige and authority by mounting an expedition in the name of the community and, using its power to call in all the manpower it needed, set about building the largest raft that had yet been seen. The selection of its 24-man crew was made according to customs long established for the raising of military expeditions, and the sailing date was fixed so as to extract the maximum propaganda value from completion of the operation shortly before the Midsummer Assembly. Difficulties arose during construction because no one had any experience of building such a big raft but the Elders would brook no delays; the work went on unceasingly despite the misgivings of the more experienced builders, who wanted more time to experiment with different techniques. The few who expressed their doubts were dismissed from the project for disloyalty and the rest remained silent. Public festivities organised to mark the launch generated a wave of enthusiasm which closed the ears of any who might have been inclined to listen to unwelcome evidence.

The tribal venture set out inauspiciously into deteriorating weather after hasty and inadequate trials. The raft broke up in heavy seas with the loss of her captain and most of her crew and passengers including the first holder of the newly created post of Overstrapper of Marine. A handful of survivors eventually returned on foot after struggling ashore some miles along the coast.

These survivors were eagerly questioned about their experiences and the fate of their comrades. They had an extraordinary tale to tell. The ocean it seemed was a hostile place, the waves had been very much larger and more powerful than they had expected, dragging at the raft, twisting and wracking it, even washing right across it and rendering it enormously much more difficult to propel and control than had the roughest rapids that anyone had encountered on the river. But what caused the greatest sensation was their allegation that they had been drugged or poisoned. Shortly after emerging from the estuary all the crew had begun to feel unwell with symptoms of dizziness, headache, lethargy and increasing nausea. Nearly all were sick, and many continued to retch miserably for hours until they became exhausted and so careless of their own survival that they made no attempt to avoid being washed overboard or to help themselves when they were in the water. Morale had completely broken down. The smallest effort, mental or physical, had seemed beyond anyone's capacity and the captain had seemed incapable of judgement or decision.

This aspect of the survivors' story came as a welcome relief to the tribal council because it diverted attention from the embarrassing questions that were being asked about their competence in planning and directing the expedition and provided them with a scapegoat. The fact that none of those who had remained ashore had been affected by the alleged drug could be explained by assuming that someone had got at the crew's waterskins, none of which had survived the accident.

Scratch was dubious about the drugging theory. He and his crew had noticed a feeling of grogginess during some of their longer practice sessions in the sea, but it hadn't persisted after they had got on shore and he suspected that it was something in the sea itself that they had either swallowed or inhaled. He questioned the survivors closely about their experiences, and came to the conclusion that the raft had been too big and unwieldy. It appeared that the crew had become tired and discouraged, and then some of the lashings had begun to fail. At first they repaired the damage as soon as it became evident but when they began to suffer from the sickness they put off the repairs, hoping that things would get better. But the damage had spread, one failure leading to another until the task had become so great they had not known where to start. The final break-up had been cataclysmal. A series of huge waves had churned the logs apart and scattered them. Some of the men had been crushed while others, exhausted, sank. The remainder clinging to logs for support had tried to swim to land, and of these all but five had perished.

When they had gathered all the information they could get out of the survivors, Scratch and his crew slipped quietly back to their encampment on the coast where their own raft was concealed. There, lying on the dry sand at the back of the beach with the distant rumble of the surf in their ears, they debated the experience of the tribal expedition and the prospects for their own.

The result of their deliberations can be summarised:

1 Given the experimental nature of the enterprise it was a mistake to aim for completion by the date of the Midsummer Assembly.

2 There were no grounds for assuming that the largest raft ever built would be suitable for the voyage, flattering though it might be to the organisers' self-esteem.

3 If either the type of raft or the time factor had been excluded from the original aim there would have been scope for flexibility and the plan would have had a better chance of succeeding.

4 The council-convened inquiry had identified the primary cause of the disaster as the incapacity of the crew following poisoning 'by persons unknown'. 'And with substances unidentified',

chorused Scratch's crew, who had a healthy contempt for official pomposity. Nevertheless they recognised an important factor here that deserved further investigation. A fit crew might have prevented the break-up of the raft and would certainly have had more survivors.

5 The captain had lost his life pressing on in the face of deteriorating weather with a sick crew and a raft showing signs of structural failure. Scratch's crew felt that he ought to have abandoned the expedition while the raft was still in a navigable condition. They had considerable sympathy for him in what was undoubtedly a difficult dilemma. After all, the organisers had impressed upon him that they had done their part, the builders had done theirs, and now it was up to him. Failure would be laid at his door. The pressure to gamble at long odds had been great, but despite the fact that to turn back would have meant the probable ruin of his career he should have done so. It was a risk that was inherent in the job. 'But', they said, 'this brings us full circle back to the aim. These pressures on the captain stem from the requirement to conclude the expedition by a certain date.'

'Which has no legitimate relevance', said Scratch.

'Lah di dah,' they said, 'what does that mean?'

'Well,' said Scratch, 'if you said you had to be back before the autumn gales, that would be relevant because if you were still out there with the sort of rafts we've got and our limited experience you'd be on a one-way trip.'

As a result of the disastrous tribal expedition Scratch and his crew introduced an extra stage into their training. This was to consist of a series of dawn-to-dusk trials along the coast, which would be repeated until they had come successfully through bad weather. For the first of these trials they set themselves the goal of rounding the furthest headland that was visible from the river mouth. Their observations had already given them an understanding of the tides which flooded into the river and raised the water level in considerably less time than it took for the ebb to fall to low water. They were also beginning to suspect that instead of the flood running straight towards the land and the ebb straight away from it, as they did in the river mouth, the streams ran to and fro more or less parallel with the coast and changed direction at quite different times.

On the first of these excursions they floated out of the river on the ebb at morning twilight and, having cleared the turbulent water on the bar, rested while Scratch took careful note of his marks on the land. Then they set off again paddling steadily over a calm sea towards the distant cliff that marked the seaward limit of a huge mountain spur. With increasing distance from the coast their progress became difficult to detect. The land seemed to stand still instead of sliding past as the river banks had done, but Scratch laid his paddle down from time to time and staring at the far-off land professed himself satisfied that they were covering the ground. After some time he exclaimed that they were going faster and must be enjoying a favourable current. It was now quite obvious even to a casual glance that the land was going past, even though a rising swell was making the work of the paddlers more difficult. Feeling the increasing size of the swell they instinctively looked at the sky, for they knew that when the swell started surging up the beaches the fine weather was often displaced within the day by clouds and wind and rain. Sure enough a steely haze of cirrus had veiled the blue so subtly that though the day still seemed bright the men found that they had lost their shadows, and there were distinct clouds over the western horizon. By noon the sun was obscured, the cloud bank in the west had grown taller and darker and little white pillows of cloud were growing on the tops of the mountains, spreading slowly down their flanks, not moving with the breeze which had sprung up from seaward but seeming to cling to the land. Scratch called a halt.

'Put up your paddles,' he said. 'Eat, drink and rest. Soon we shall have a good trial.'

When they resumed paddling it was harder work, drizzle had started to fall and the wind which had shifted rather more to the left of the line of the swells was beginning to raise a sea whose crests slopped over the raft. All the land down to the cliff-tops was now covered in cloud, and detail was becoming obscured by the drizzle.

The men plied their paddles in silence, feeling muzzy and abstracted. Some turned a bad colour, in particular two who had not eaten during the noon break, the normally rhythmic paddle strokes became ragged.

'Come on, get it together', said Scratch and started a paddling chant which the crew picked up, swinging their shoulders in unison and hefting great puddles of water aft along the raft sides. For a time they recovered their spirits and after the song was ended there was some exchange of banter but it was not long before silence returned and each retreated into the solitary monotony of his labour.

They were not greatly concerned when rain and clouds shut out the last sight of land. At least fifty generations of their descendants would pass before anyone would see a chart or a compass, yet they felt perfectly secure in their instinctive sense of direction. Their orientation was as continuous and unconscious as their breathing, all the time gathering directional information both crude and subtle from their surroundings: they never questioned 'which way', they just pointed their noses and went. Even though the storm cut him off from most of his familiar natural pointers, Scratch knew where the land lay and knew that he could find it even in pitch darkness. But as he watched the raft twisting and wallowing in the seas he felt a first clutch of alarm. His knowledge of direction was no longer enough; he could not bring the raft to land in such a sea unless he could find a sheltered place with relatively smooth water: to attempt a landing on the rocky headland to leeward would result in raft and men being smashed to pieces. He suddenly realised that he was in danger of losing the initiative. Circumstances were taking control and his mind seemed to choke on a confusion of alternatives, turning wildly from one to another without getting a proper grasp on any of them.

To steady himself he called a halt and split the crew into two shifts, ordering half of them to rest and the others to paddle gently, keeping the raft head-on to the seas. Most of the men were seasick and all were tired with the double effort of paddling and maintaining their positions in the rough sea. He distributed the spare lashing vines to the resting watch and told each man to secure first his opposite number who was paddling and then himself.

Meanwhile he considered the alternatives:

1 They could go on round the headland where the changing direction of the coast held out some hope of their finding a sheltering indentation. It was a gamble but attractive because it allowed them to maintain the original aim, a positive action good for flagging crew morale.
2 Return to the river. A long way and a retreat at that. The crew would be very tired. It would be dark by the time they got there and might be difficult to identify if the visibility failed to improve. Unless they approached on the flood, the sea in the entrance would be dangerous in this onshore wind. The only advantage was that of familiarity. The devil you knew, in fact.
3 Conserve crew strength and sea room by keeping head to sea and paddling just enough not to lose ground. Provided the weather did not get much worse or go on too long the raft and crew would probably hang together.

Option 2 was clearly ruled out. The choice lay between 1 and 3. He reconsidered them and saw at once that the key to the whole problem lay in retaining the initiative and that the apparent advantages of sticking to the original plan and of maintaining crew morale were illusory since both aims could be achieved by other means. He perceived that his advantage lay in maintaining an offing and knew that he could do this if the crew could keep going and if the raft remained intact. To close the land would be to risk that advantage on the uncertainty of finding shelter. Once inshore they would not have the strength to regain sea room.

'This can't last forever and the raft is standing up fine', he said.

'We'll just heave-to until the weather clears.'

Well, they were lucky. That evening a furious squall lashed them with hail and spray and for a few minutes the raft was totally unmanageable. Then a deluge of rain flattened the sea and obliterated everything until it too passed and they saw blue sky, the horizon cleared to seaward and parts of the coast began to emerge from below a huge wall of cloud as the occlusion retreated inland. They saw with something of a shock that they had been driven to within a mile of the headland but the wind had now veered and was blowing parallel with the coast, whipping up white horses everywhere except in the lee of the headland where they saw the entrance to a sheltered bay.

Neither Scratch nor any of his contemporaries ever made it to Yonderland. The invention of the paddle had not been enough. The rafts were too heavy and unwieldy for the strength of their crews. A new technical breakthrough was needed. Scratch stumbled on the seed of it when he was making a toy raft for the children. Finding the tiny lashings for the twigs too fiddly he bound them in a single piece cut from an old waterskin and suddenly realised that if he rearranged the twigs in the form of a frame he could discard most of them and more than halve the weight. He had invented the skin boat. The next two stages of progress—devising the construction of a light but strong frame hull, and joining skins together in a watertight manner—were not completed in his lifetime.

Once the true boat had come into being the tribesmen's radius of action increased spectacularly and with the invention of the sail really long voyages became possible; experience was broadened, contact with other cultures led to the exchange of ideas and the acceleration of all forms of technical progress right down to our day. But although the technical aspects attract attention the basic concerns of the modern seaman are the same as those of his distant ancestors who set out from the river mouth on their simple rafts. First there is the natural arena in which he operates: the sea and the protruding patches of the earth's crust on which he must depend, together with its envelope of atmosphere. Second come the human actors, the skippers and crews with their aims, their qualities of character and intellect, their physical capabilities and limitations. Finally the means through which these aims are achieved, the boats and their equipment together with the methods by which they are managed and handled.

We shall be returning to the experiences of Scratch and his friends, but let us look first at the harsh, destructive, often beautiful and always fascinating world in which the seaman works.

3
The Sea

3

Waves

To our ancestral raftmen the first and most striking feature of the sea was its wave-covered surface. They were impressed when they saw it from the land, even more so when the inert logs of the raft began pressing up underneath them like the backs of live beasts, and when later those same logs that they could scarcely lift began to be tossed about like straws they must have been amazed and terrified at such power. On first acquaintance one wave seems to be much like another, threatening to rear up and pour salt water over you or to take the deck from under you and unship your stomach from its moorings; but each is different, different now to what it was before and what it will become, different from another whose origins and history are not the same, different here to what it would be in another place. A knowledge of waves enables the seaman to avoid the worst of their consequences and also to use the information they carry.

The sea is affected by several different kinds of wave, but by far the most common are waves raised by the wind, which are called *sea*, and those which continue after the wind has ceased or has changed direction and which are known as *swell.* Although sea and swell behave differently the waves composing them have the same features and characteristics.

Form

The profiles of waves vary considerably as they are composed of several theoretical wave forms in different combinations. The most usual for a wind-driven wave approximates to the path traced out by a point inside the rim of a wheel running along the underside of a level surface: it is characterised by relatively peaked crests and more gently curving troughs, while ocean swells tend to have a more symmetrical form with rounded, convex crests.

Motion

There are two quite different kinds of motion in a wave: the *motion of matter* in which particles of water describe a small almost circular vertical orbit at low speed with only a minute resultant change of position; and the *motion of motion* in which the wave form moves progressively along the surface of the water at much higher speeds. As this progressive movement involves no matter it is uninfluenced by the Coriolis effect, which deflects winds and currents into curved paths, and wave motion tends to continue in its original direction.

Dimensions

The horizontal distance in the direction of travel between two successive crests is called *length*. The vertical distance from trough to crest is known as *height*. The time interval between the passage of successive crests past a fixed point is the *period* (Fig 1). Length and period determine speed, and in a theoretical wave have a mathematical relationship. Height has no constant relationship to the other dimensions, but all three depend upon the strength of the wind, the time it has been blowing in a given direction, and its *fetch*, the distance it has been blowing in a straight line over the sea.

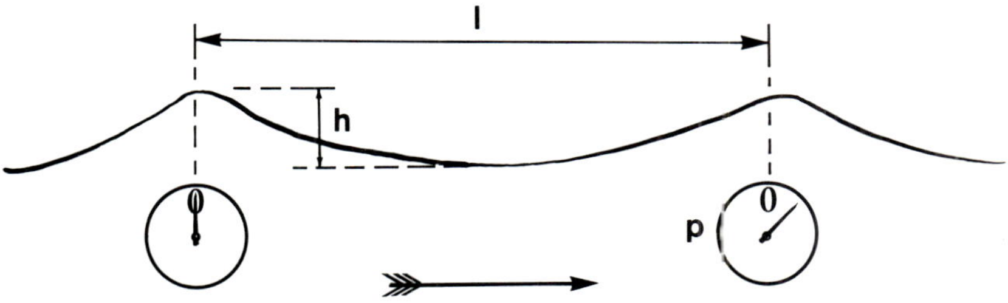

Fig 1 Wave length and height: *h* = height; *l* = length; *p* = period of wave

Formation of Sea

When a wind starts to blow it raises small waves on the surface of the sea. As time goes on these waves get higher and longer, and their period increases. At first height increases more rapidly than do length and period but, as height approaches the limit for the wind strength and fetch it stabilises, while period and length continue to increase. The effect of this is that seas become steeper while they are growing but go on getting longer and faster for a time after they have reached full height. If the wind increases again the process is repeated and the greater and more rapid the increase in wind the steeper do the seas become.

Formation of Swell

When the wind stops blowing or changes direction, the sea it caused continues to travel on as swell. As long as it remains in water that is deeper than half the wave length it is considered to be in *deep water* and its length preserves the relationship to its period given by the formula

$$L = 1{\cdot}56\ P^2$$

where L is the length in metres, and P is the period in seconds. As period can be measured reasonably accurately by timing the passage of crests past a buoy or even a patch of foam, the length, which is extremely difficult to estimate, can be calculated. As the speed in knots of a swell wave in deep water is for practical purposes three times the period in seconds we can give some values to the sort of waves that are likely in summer off the Atlantic coasts of Europe (see table).

Without the energy of the wind to sustain them the waves of a swell gradually decrease in height, but their period and length continue to increase, although at a diminishing rate: they thus become less obvious but move faster as they travel away from their original area.

If the wave system as a whole advanced at the speed of individual waves it would provide an almost infallible warning of the approach of strong winds, but as each leading wave in turn is 'eaten' by its successors, which absorb its energy (the process can be observed clearly in the washes of ships passing through smooth water), the group of waves in an area of swell advances at half the speed of the individual waves which comprise it. The arrival of a swell is always worth remarking and, if a note is made of its direction and period, subsequent alteration can be observed and added to other evidence about its possible origins and their development.

Table showing the lengths and speeds of swell waves of different periods in water deeper than half the wave length.

Period (seconds)	Length (metres)	Speed (knots)
4	25	12
5	39	15
6	56	18
7	76	21
8	100	24
9	126	27
10	156	30
11	189	33
12	225	36

Effect of Shoal Water

When a wave enters water less deep than half the wave length it begins to feel the interference of the sea bed. Its length decreases without alteration to its period, so it goes more slowly, while its height, after an initial slight decrease, begins to increase rapidly with decreasing depth. This causes the swell to become shorter and steeper, and can be quite dramatic when an old far-travelled swell, that has become so low and long as to be barely noticeable, encounters a shoal and suddenly humps up to form a huge rolling sea. The longer swells of the North Atlantic enter critical depths as they approach the crest of the continental rise which, in the Biscay region, lies along the track of ships crossing the bay and is largely responsible for the notoriety of the area among sea travellers. Seas and shorter swells from lesser distances or smaller disturbances reach the critical half wave length depth in shallower water. If the period is known the table shown above can be used to find this depth. The length and speed of seas is somewhat less than those of swells in proportion to period but if the same figures are used the error will be on the safe side.

When the depth of water falls to one-tenth of the deep-water wave length the increase of height becomes very marked, the progressive deceleration causes crowding with steepening and narrowing of the crests, retardation of the troughs steepens the wave fronts more than their backs and the wave is ready to break at the least provocation. At a depth equal to one-twenty-fifth of the deep-water wave length the relationship between length and period disappears, the wave's speed becomes dependent on depth alone and it breaks.

Sudden shoaling can cause a wave to break in any depth once it has entered water less than half its wave length deep, and swells may break over rocks 20 metres below the surface. In waters where unmarked rocks abound, pilotage is made easier when there is enough swell to break on them.

Refraction

It seldom happens that the fronts of advancing waves are parallel to the bottom contours, so one side of the wave reaches its critical depth and begins to slow down before the rest with a result similar to optical refraction.

Refraction causes the swells to swing round and align themselves with the bottom contours. The longest swells which reach their critical depths first, display the most pronounced tendency to set four-square towards the adjacent coast, a characteristic which 'primitive' navigators have found useful. Modern mariners, equipped with compasses and other sophisticated devices, can still profit from a knowledge of wave refraction because it causes waves to converge on ridges and to diverge from submarine valleys. Hence waves may focus and produce crossing systems near headlands or ridge-type shoals, and spread away from the centres of bays to leave comparatively smooth areas while the shores are turbulent with waves arriving from several different directions.

Interference

With changes of wind generating new wave systems, old seas becoming swells, seas and swells changing their lengths and being refracted it will be understood that sea and swell are never as simple as the ideal waves of theory, and very rarely do they consist of a single system of waves. Waves frequently cross and even when they travel in the same direction their different characteristics blend to give results that do not appear in either system alone. When the difference in length is pronounced, as commonly occurs when a sea is meeting or being overtaken by an old swell, the two component waves retain their identities. But when waves of only slightly different period and length combine they produce groups of noticeably higher waves interspersed at fairly regular intervals with groups of remarkably lower ones as the component waves move in and out of phase.

Another type of interference occurs when waves reach a vertical cliff or breakwater and are reflected. The reflected wave leaves the wall at the same angle as that at which it arrived (exactly as light does) and retains its characteristics. If the angle of approach is square the incident and reflected waves collide to cause a standing wave that can be of great violence. If the angle of approach is oblique a cross sea is formed.

Effect of Currents

Currents exert a powerfully modifying influence upon waves, lengthening them when they are travelling in the same direction and shortening them when they are opposed. As we shall see later, currents have an unexpectedly potent effect on the energy of the apparent wind so their effect on sea is more marked than it is on swell. With a lee-going tide the steepness of the seas is reduced not only by their increased length but also by the lowering of their height because of the diminished wind energy. With a weather-going stream the increased wind pressure raises the height of the sea, and because it is exerted more on the crests than on the troughs, steepens their faces more than their backs and produces a characteristically concave or hollow sea with curling crests. A weather-going tide of 2 to 3 knots can cause seas to break. A current setting obliquely across waves affects them in proportion to its favourable or adverse components. Current at right angles have little effect when they are weak, but strong ones such as exist in tide races can obliterate a sea and create an area of smooth water to leeward as long as the stream is running. Some apparently exposed inlets afford safe anchorage because the tidal streams that run across their entrances prevent any sea from penetrating, and the period of slack water does not last long enough for a sea to develop, although a swell may be felt during this time.

Breakers

When the crest of a sea becomes unstable, either because of the effect of shallow water or because of the force of the wind, it breaks and surfs down the face of the wave. In doing so it accelerates from a knot or two at most to the speed of the wave, which could be of the order of 30 knots. For a given speed the energy of a breaking crest depends on how much solid water, as opposed to air and water, it contains, but with sea water at a ton per cubic metre even a modest, well-aerated crest produces a clout equivalent to collision with a small car.

Because of the lowered density of broken water a boat cannot rise to it as she does to a wave and it pours over her. On meeting resistance the broken water promptly expels its air and becomes capable of floating objects, such as crew members, which it takes along with it if they are unsecured. The boat meanwhile is pressed down by the burden of water on her decks into solid and relatively slow-moving water. Her ability to survive depends on the strength and watertightness of her hull and deck, and her ability to yield bodily to the moving mass of water.

Planning and Handling

The sheer size of a wave is no guide to its menace. The crew of the smallest boat can negotiate the highest waves without a tremor provided that they are long and therefore not steep. Steepness causes violent motion, hampers the performance of both boat and crew and renders the sea liable to break. Heavy breaking seas are even more detrimental to performance and can inflict injuries unsurpassed by any other agency except solid ground, other vessels or ice: clearly we should try to avoid them.

The waves we meet at sea are rarely simple: usually there are several systems of waves of different length moving in different directions. The shallower the water the more of them will be in depths less than half their wave lengths. Thus in rough weather there is advantage in keeping in water deeper than the critical depth of as many of these waves as possible. Also to be avoided are places where the bottom contours cause waves to converge by refraction, areas of strong weathergoing currents, and the proximity of steep coasts, even if the water is deep.

If breaking seas are encountered the security of the crew on deck is the first consideration. A good sized dollop of water travelling at 20 knots can knock a man off his feet, and if there is enough of it to half-float him he will be washed away, so safety harnesses are essential. Similarly all gear on deck must be securely stowed with special attention to sails. Nothing exposes the inadequate stowage of a sail as surely as a few seas washing over it, and there is hardly a nastier job than to have to re-stow it under such conditions.

Whether to take breaking seas on the bow, the beam or on the stern, depends more than anything on the individual boat. Some like it one way, some another. The advantage of running is that the boat frequently surfs in the crests which consequently overtake slowly and, although the surge of the breakers may run level with her gunwales and even spill over the decks, they do so without great violence. As there is no difficulty in keeping up her speed she is under good control and can be turned to take the ones that come at odd angles. It can be trying for the helmsman, who needs a steady nerve and good concentration, and some boats are too demanding, but a boat that will run steadily should be able to handle a normal summer gale. Should she broach, however, she will come virtually to a stop and if there is a breaking sea coming up it will sweep her at the full speed of its advance.

Sometimes it may be necessary to take the sea on the bow in order to preserve sea room or to avoid conceding hard-won distance to windward, and some boats have a weakness aft in the design of the cockpit or the superstructure that makes this course advisable. Close-hauled the motion is more violent but it is the point of sailing on which the boat will be most likely to sail herself under easy canvas without attention and so, if her speed can be kept low enough, is easiest on her crew.

Tides and Currents

The movement of the tides has always been something of a mystery. It must have been a dominant influence in the lives of those early coastal dwellers whose kitchen middens record the extent to which they relied on shellfish, and the first navigators could not have failed to note in most parts of the world the correspondence between the rhythms of the tides and those of the moon. Convincing explanation of the phenomena, however, and the development of a theory capable of providing a practical link between regular astronomical events and the mystifyingly complex behaviour of the waters of the oceans long proved elusive.

The well-known theory of the difference in the combined gravitational attraction of the sun and moon at different points on the surface of the spinning earth is fine in the classroom, and would accord nicely with the observed behaviour of the oceans if the rough edges of the earth had been cleaned up to allow the water to stand 2 miles deep all over the globe without interruption. For the fact is that the bumps and hollows of the earth's crust that divide the oceans into separate basins, and protrude through their surface here and there to form the patches of land that give us our tenuous foothold, so distort results that the cause is scarcely discernible. In different places, not always far apart, the tide does different things. There can be one, two or four high and low waters in each 24-hour period; the heights of successive tides can be almost equal in one place, and in another so dissimilar that on the same day the higher low water is almost as high as the lower high water; in different parts of the British Isles alone the spring range of the tide varies from less than 1 metre to more than 12. The shortest acquaintance with the sea is enough for it to become apparent that horizontal streams only rarely change direction in unison with the rising and falling of the tide. But there are other anomalies. The stream can run longer in one direction than it does in the other, slack water can occur in an estuary at a time when the level of water is changing most rapidly, and in the Sound of Harris not only does the tide at neaps run one way by day and another by night, regardless of whether the tide is rising or falling, but the directions are reversed between summer and winter. Of course there are explanations, but I shall not try to give them here because the ordinary mariner can make no practical use of them but must be guided by the tide tables and the Pilots whose information comes from observation and not conjecture.

The vertical movement of the tides is a subject well suited to the classroom, well covered by shore-based courses with ample exercise in the computation of heights at different states of the tide; and since it is necessary to discover the height of the tide before you can interpret a chart or drop an anchor there is small chance of the knowledge becoming rusty through lack of use. Eventually it becomes a drill: you assemble the information and do the sum and, unless the wind is strong enough or the barometric pressure unusual enough to make an adjustment necessary, that is it. Tidal streams, however, need a somewhat different approach. The information concerning them is both more scanty and more scattered, the factors affecting the strength and direction at a given time and place more varied, and there is more need for interpretation and judgement.

The most useful information about tidal streams is to be found in the Pilots. The streams are often described in detail, the times at which they begin and end are given more precisely than is shown on the chart, and there is often information about inshore streams which appears nowhere else. Pocket Tidal Stream Atlases present a useful overall graphic picture that is particularly convenient for planning, both before the passage and during it when you want to look ahead and see how the situation is developing. The presentation of the most recent editions is so clear that it is easy to add additional information such as inshore streams, eddies and races, together with more precise timings of events, most of which will have been found in the Pilot and some derived from local experience. This enables all the information to be seen at a glance without the need to refer to different books.

It is useful to remember that the tidal stream is only one component of the total horizontal movement of water. Being the one that reverses periodically, and usually being the stronger in coastal waters it may mask the existence of wind-driven currents which nevertheless exist and exert their modifying influence, especially at neap tides when the streams are weaker and the period of slack water longer. A wind that has been blowing for twelve hours creates a current about 2 per cent of the wind speed, so a 25 knot wind produces a $\frac{1}{2}$ knot current which, if parallel to a tide of $1\frac{1}{2}$ knots, would cause it to run at 2 knots in one direction and 1 in the other. The direction of a wind-driven current is deflected like the wind itself to the right in the northern hemisphere and to the left in the southern. Surprisingly for a surface current, the angle of deflection increases with depth of water as well as the latitude to a maximum of 45°, while 15° is usual in shallow coastal waters in temperate latitudes.

In coastal waters significant differences in sea level can exist over short horizontal distances because of the difference in tidal range or of the times of high and low water. The resulting slope in the sea surface can cause much more powerful currents than might be expected from the local tidal range. Thus, although the mean range of the tide between Islay and Kintyre is only a $\frac{1}{2}$ metre and barely discernible, that to the west of Islay and to the east of Kintyre is five times as great and the region abounds in strong tides with heavy races. Similar effects occur elsewhere with smaller height differences.

Working the tides to maximum advantage is an interesting and satisfying exercise when coasting. The earlier times at which the streams inshore usually turn and the higher rates normally attained by them in the vicinity of headlands has led to the useful rule of standing inshore at the end of the foul tide and offshore at the end of the fair tide, and of aiming to pass headlands with the fair tide and bays on the foul one. The rule should not, however, be followed blindly and without regard to the capacity of currents to affect seas and apparent wind. These are discussed in the chapters on waves and wind.

Tide Races

Tidal races are mainly coastal phenomena, found wherever the smooth advance of tidal water is deflected or concentrated in the vicinity of islands, shoals, straits and major headlands; just those very points on which seamen converge when coasting or making their landfalls. They can vary from a small patch of ripples to an area of 50 square miles or more of heavily breaking seas, and they are so much affected by the state of tide, sea and wind that at different times the same race can be negotiated in safety by the smallest boat or inflict severe damage on a ship. On one occasion an offing of a couple of miles may take you clear outside a race in undisturbed water, on another 10 miles may be inadequate and you could wish yourself twice as far away.

There was a time when a yacht on coastal passage could plan to pass the major headlands at a distance great enough to clear the races at their greatest extent yet near enough for visual fixing, but now that traffic separation schemes have been established off many of the major race-producing headlands the yachtsman has to make the decision, usually many hours in advance whether to pass these headlands at a distance that will take him close to the races and even through them under certain conditions, or to make a wide detour and avoid the area altogether. In making this decision the need to recognise 'favourable conditions' and demonstrate 'proper management' is as urgent as any that a small-boat sailor has to face.

The location, extent and behaviour of individual races are described, often in great detail, in the Admiralty Pilots, which should always be consulted before approaching the area in order to judge the best course to follow and most advantageous timing of the passage. But if the best use is to be made of this information it is necessary to understand something of the anatomy of races in general and their response to all the variable factors of wind and weather.

The purely tidal effects of a race can best be understood by first considering the behaviour of the water in a river too small for the formation of large wind-generated waves. The bit we want to look at is the place where a shoal causes a stretch of minor rapids between two deep placid reaches. The water in the upper reach slips along smooth and undisturbed except for the light stippling of the breeze, its motion discernible only by the passage of the suspended silt particles and objects floating on its surface. As it nears the restriction at the head of the rapids it accelerates, becoming at first glassy, as the surface ceases to respond to wind pressure, and then longitudinally striated. Vortices and whirlpools may form. Outcrops on the sides and bed of the channel produce V-shaped wash-waves, humps and wakes, and an oily undulation develops into a series of low standing waves which, moving against the current at a speed but little below that of the stream itself, appear almost stationary. On a river this stage is known as the 'glide', and though the surface is not level it is characteristically smooth and glassy: it is devoid of angularity except locally at the origin of the occasional wash-wave which quickly becomes rounded and then flattened.

As we are looking for clues to the behaviour of navigable sea our model rapids are but lightly obstructed and no extreme turbulence develops over the shoal. What we see is a progressive increase in height of the standing waves until the water deepens towards the tail of the shoal. Here the standing waves are still roller-like and rounded but progressively higher and steeper until they become unstable and break on a line which marks the transition to the overfalls. The next few waves , though hollow, frequently retain the long form and parallel organisation of the rollers at the bottom of the glide, and may break simultaneously across a wide front. In the body of the race order soon gives way to chaos as hollow, breaking waves lurch and topple this way and that, collide, rebound, mount one upon another and collapse in foam and tumult.

In contrast to its abrupt beginning, the race peters out gradually; the waves subside leaving only a swell which spreads radially outwards from the disturbance which caused it. Downstream of the race lies another zone of turbulence utterly different in character. Here the surface is domed and dimpled by currents that run in all directions, wheeling, dividing, coalescing, welling up from the depths, diving down again under a lip of spume. Apart from a few patches of ripples at the margin of eddies, the general appearance of this final stage is rounded but pockmarked. Oily rather than glassy, it resists the formation of wind ripples. In the downstream reach the disturbance finally disappears in a residual swell.

Tidal races are more complex and variable than this rather simple model, but the same basic structure is there, energised in proportion to the strength of the stream and interacting in each of its parts with wind, sea and swell.

Effect of Wind

The wind often becomes noticeably stronger when entering a tide race. Opposition of wind and tide creates an increase in the apparent wind, and as the tidal velocity is usually higher in races than in the surrounding sea, this increase can be marked. But it sometimes occurs when wind and tide are together, and may be caused by the topography which causes the race, also accelerating the wind, or to mechanical and thermal turbulence in the water producing a corresponding turbulence in the air. Any component of wind against tide is an unfavourable factor because it increases the height and steepness of the sea and its tendency to break.

Effect of Sea

Being the direct product of wind, modified by tide, the state of the sea can be observed or estimated. A race acts as a breakwater so that an area in its lee where the sea is rough at slack water may become smooth while the race is running. In the area upstream of the race corresponding to the river's glide, the sea is less than elsewhere in the race and, provided that there is no appreciable component of wind against tide, it may be smoother here than it is clear of the race. Given that inadequate way may result in your being drawn into the overfalls, this is the best place in which to cross a race whose streams lie athwart your course. In the race itself the tendency will be for the pattern of sea to be obliterated in the chaos of overfalls, but its weight will be added to the confusion. The 'tail' of swirls and eddies will normally be distinguishable only in quiet weather: if there is any sea this area will be covered with patches of turbulence and overfalls and appear as an extension of the body of the race.

Effect of Swell

The collision between a race and a heavy swell is devastating. Since a swell may be imperceptible on the upstream side of a race, and since the absence of swell cannot be inferred from lack of wind, great caution is needed when passing from sheltered water to the open sea through a sound that has a race in its entrance. Swell can so far outrun its parent disturbance that prevailing good weather is no reliable guarantee of its absence on an exposed coast. Before embarking on the passage of a race whose further end could be encountering swell, you need either confirmation of reasonable conditions or an escape route. Where there is an anchorage as conveniently placed as Stromness is to Hoy Sound you can take a short walk to the top of a hill and see for yourself. Elsewhere you might telephone someone such as a lighthouse keeper or coastguard who can see what conditions are like. Or you could ask someone who has come in from outside. If you can do none of these things you can time your passage of the race for the slack water preceding the start of the incoming stream, when the race will be quiet and you can still turn and flee should you not care for the look of it. In these conditions, applying the normally seamanlike principle of starting with the first of the fair tide may leave you with no option but to go forward.

Summarising the effects of these influences on races we can say that conditions are ameliorated by:

1 *Slack water*: (time relative to local high water usually given in the Admiralty Pilot) There may be a period of no race around slack water.
2 *Neap tides*: Extent, duration and violence of race least.
3 *Lee-going tide*: Less apparent wind; sea lower and less steep.
4 *Light winds*: Smoother sea; race less extensive.
5 *Settled weather*: Less likelihood of swell.

Conditions are exacerbated by:

1 *Spring tides*: Greatest extent and violence of race; short or non-existent period of slack.
2 *Weather-going tide*: More apparent wind; sea higher and steeper.
3 *Strong winds*: Rough sea; area of race extends.
4 *Swell*.

Action

Having assembled all the evidence, estimate the likely conditions and plan the best time and course for the passage. If intending to avoid the race, the worse the conditions the wider the berth you will need to give it and the greater the chance that any inshore passage will be non-existent or unapproachable. When making the passage of an unfamiliar race try to arrange the timing that will give you a combination of favourable circumstances and an absence of unfavourable ones. Be prepared for a change of wind because of funnelling or the effect of tide. In the event of an involuntary passage of a race of which you lack previous experience, expect to be thrown around violently and, even if your boat is normally buoyant and dry, to take large quantities of green water on deck and over the superstructure, and for pitching to become so violent that the boat may lose steerage way and deck work become impossible. Anticipate this by changing to high clewed headsails that will not scoop up the sea and, if the wind is forward of the beam, adjust sail area to allow for the increase of apparent wind. Secure everything on deck and below. Close all openings into the hull, put on harnesses, and if you like fish now is the time to put out the line. The quickest route out of a race is usually straight down tide but it is sometimes possible in daylight to avoid the worst of the overfalls. Keeping track of your position in the strong erratic currents and disturbing circumstances of a tide race can be difficult unless thorough preparation has been made and the pilot thinks ahead.

The Coriolis Effect

What follows is strictly for the non-mathematical unscientific reader, the sort of person whose mind like mine shrivels like an overdried walnut when required to visualise 'a direction perpendicular both to the axis of the earth and to the velocity of a body relative to the earth, such that a positive rotation about it carries the earth's axis towards the direction of relative velocity'. If you can contemplate that sentence without reeling, if two omega vee sine phi makes sense to you, and if an invitation to consider the earth as a rotating disc does not put you in mind of a con man's opening gambit you had better skip to the next chapter because what follows will tell you nothing new and may merely irritate you as the mental fumbling of a duffer.

The surface of the earth slopes down from the equator to the pole through a vertical distance of about 12 nautical miles which is equivalent to a mean slope of 13 feet in every mile. To us, however, and our spirit levels and plumb lines, the surface appears level, and the oceans whose mean depth is about 2 nautical miles show no tendency to flow down to the poles and stand there 12 miles deep while leaving the equator high and dry. For just as every pebble and every grain of sand on a sloping beach occupies its natural level on the slope in accordance with its size, so every object on the face of the earth occupies its appropriate place on its sloping surface according to its speed of rotation round the earth's axis. If you move one of the pebbles and put it where it does not match its neighbours in size it will find its way back to its proper level: the pebble might tell you that the surface of the beach seems to it to be horizontal only in this region and to slope upwards both above and below it. As long as you remain stationary you occupy your rightful place on the sloping surface of the spinning earth because your speed of rotation exactly matches that of your surroundings, but as soon as you move you upset this balance. If you happen to have a spirit level about you it will tell you that the surface beneath you is no longer horizontal, and you will have a tendency to wander off in search of a new balance between latitude and speed of rotation. The big difference between you and the pebble is that while the pebble's size is constant your velocity is dependent on direction and so is continually changing even when your measured speed remains the same.

If you find it difficult to visualise this connection between latitude and speed of rotation it may help if we imagine what would happen if the earth's speed of rotation were to be changed. Speeding up the spin would cause us, together with all other loose objects and fluids, to drift towards the equator and pile up there in a heap: our spirit levels would have told us that the surface sloped downwards that way. Slowing down the spin would cause the reverse to happen. Of course the earth itself would tend to distort as well, becoming more flattened or more spherical according to whether the rate of spin increased or decreased, and if it were elastic enough to adjust itself completely the surface would seem to us to remain level and we should have no tendency to wander away from our resting places.

Moving over the surface towards the east increases our speed of rotation, but the slope which is correct for the earth—and for us when we are at rest—is too little for our new speed and so we swerve towards the equator. Movement in a westerly direction decreases our speed of rotation so we descend towards the pole. Moving towards or away from the pole makes our initial velocity towards the east respectively higher or lower than that of the surface over which we are moving. We end up having either overtaken or lagged behind its eastward motion.

The earth rotates towards the east with a surface speed of approximately 900 knots at the equator, decreasing to zero at the poles, and regardless of where we are or in what direction we are moving we can think of our motion as being faster when it is towards the east, slower towards the equator and downhill towards the nearer pole. With this frame of reference imagine you are a big drowsy lump of perfectly still air basking in the sunshine in the northern part of the Azores anticyclone: though you have no motion relative to the earth you are travelling with it at about 600 knots to the east. Falling atmospheric pressure to the north sets you in motion, drawing you poleward over a surface whose eastward motion is ever decreasing so that your initially northward path curves to the right ahead of the surface in proportion as your east-going 600 knots exceeds the lower speed of the surface in the higher latitudes into which you are moving.

Having no further need for the pressure gradient that set you in motion, we will allow it to disappear while you coast on under your own momentum. As your motion now has an easterly component, you continue as long as you retain any movement relative to the earth to be going too fast for the latitude in which you find yourself, so you tend to drift back towards the equator and the position on the slope which accords with your speed of rotation. But this restful state can only be reached when you have come to a dead stop relative to the surface. As long as you keep moving over the surface in any direction your *actual* speed is always changing and at any given moment your latitude has to be wrong. Thus as you move towards the equator the surface is moving faster in an easterly direction to give your motion a westerly and therefore negative component which requires you to move to higher latitudes again.

If we go back to the shape of the earth and spirit levels, we see that when we are stationary the spirit level tells us that the surface of the earth is horizontal, although astronomical measurement shows it to slope down towards the poles and be truly level only at the equator. When we move, however, the spirit level tells us that regardless of which way we are going our 'horizontal' slopes to the right in the northern hemisphere and to the left in the southern. This is no empty analogy but literal fact: the artificial horizon in an aircraft sextant, which is a form of spirit level, gives a spurious reading which has to be corrected according to latitude and aircraft speed.

The practical importance of the Coriolis effect is that all moving objects have a tendency to swerve to the right in the northern hemisphere and to the left in the southern. Winds, currents, drifting ice, projectiles are all affected. The water level at one bank of a river is little higher than on the other because of this tendency, but you should not rely on being able to tell which hemisphere you are in by consulting the vortex of your vanishing bath water because the force may be masked by random influences like the shape of the bath or which foot you led with when getting out.

4
The Weather

4

Nothing commands the attention of the seaman so unremittingly as weather. Like a wild creature whose ears, eyes and nostrils are constantly on the move, testing its surroundings for the approach of prey or predators, awake and asleep he keeps a part of his mind continually alert for the signs that accompany the activity of the atmosphere. Nothing else has the power to transform in a few hours the benign playground in which he relaxes, without a care, to the grim arena in which he struggles for life. Weather raises the seaman's hopes, blights his prospects, makes the same coast a sight to fill him with gladness or with terror. The ancients sought to deserve the favour of the gods; modern man strives to understand and anticipate the processes of nature.

Using Forecasts

Forecasting the weather is essentially a process of extrapolation in which past events and present trends are projected forward to future developments. Accuracy depends on there being ample and reliable information, on the skill with which it is interpreted, and the absence of unexpected or unforeseeable events. Since the middle of the twentieth century the amount and quality of information available, the techniques of forecasting and the means of communication have improved so much that it is exceptional for anyone on land or sea to have to rely on his own unaided judgement; and with forecasts being broadcast several times a day there is a tendency for us to pay less attention to the events that are going on around us than our fathers did. This may be the result of a misguided sense of modesty. 'Weather forecasting is a job for highly trained experts' we say. 'Who are we with our rudimentary knowledge and the little evidence that we can gather, to set our opinions alongside the official forecast?' The answer may be found in the way the forecast is put together and the form in which it is disseminated, for it not only invites interpretation but cannot be used properly if it is merely taken at face value.

The first thing to be grasped about a broadcast forecast is that it is limited not by what the forecaster can tell you but by the time the broadcasting authority is prepared to give to it. In five minutes the forecast for shipping gives a synopsis of the situation on which the forecast was based, the forecasts for the next twenty-four hours for sea areas extending over threequarters of a million square miles, and the reports of actual conditions at a dozen coastal stations. The time allotted to the forecast is the same whether the situation is a simple one, with few features to be mentioned in the synopsis and widespread areas of similar weather in which little change is expected, or a complex one with several features moving rapidly through the area and giving rise to many changes. In the first instance the forecaster may have enough time to include everything he can usefully say, in the second he will have to decide on what is most important and compress or omit the rest.

Much effort has been put into making good use of the limited time available for forecasts by careful phrasing and precise terminology. The adverbs qualifying the speed at which weather features move, and the timing of expected events, the adjectives describing weight of precipitation and range of visibility all have precise meanings which need to be known if the forecast is to be properly understood. We can do more to offset the deficiencies of one type of forecast if we put together the evidence of others together with our own first-hand observations.

Land forecasts make valuable contributions to the evidence of shipping forecasts. Not only are land forecasts generally more appropriate to inshore waters but, because they concern themselves with smaller areas and a shorter time span, they have a higher probability of accuracy and are usually more specific about the timing of events. The few words at the end which give the prospects for the outlook period are particularly valuable because they may reveal significant changes beyond the end of the shipping forecast period. Thus, when we hear of 'more continuous rain or drizzle moving into the south west later on Thursday', we may not care two hoots if it rains or not and we may not even be in the south west but we are unlikely to be indifferent to the windshifts and changes in visibility that accompany it and affect a much wider area.

In order to make full use of all this information it is necessary to compare the forecast developments with the observations of actual events at coastal stations as well as those occurring in your own vicinity, and to relate the information contained in the land forecasts, making allowances for local geography. The process is the same as navigating in that it consists of four stages:

1 Assembling the evidence.
2 Reconciling the discrepancies.
3 Reaching a conclusion.
4 Assessing the reliability of the conclusion.

The last three steps are possible only if you have an understanding of basic meteorology and are aware of the weather processes that are going on around you. The theory of meteorology is interesting but not easy, and progress is greatly helped if it is possible to study a synoptic chart daily for a year or so, while at the same time observing local weather sequences including wind, cloud types, visibility, precipitation and barometric pressure. When once you know what the forecaster is talking about and you begin to think ahead you should try to amplify or modify the forecast; for example, if a front is expected, decide when, and then compare your own conclusions, as well as the forecast, with what actually happens. With perseverence and a bit of effort to see where and why you were wrong you will gain confidence in both the forecast and your own judgement.

There is no one so apt to complain that the forecast is more often wrong than right than the man who listens to and takes at face value the forecast for his local area alone while ignoring the rest and paying no heed to the evidence of his own eyes. Meteorologically such a man lives from one forecast to the next, absorbing barely enough nourishment to tide him over the interval, and never building up the experience and judgement that would enable him to compete with unexpected developments or the failure of his radio.

Water in the Atmosphere

Weather owes its existence to the air's remarkable capacity for absorbing and holding water, and to the equally remarkable capacity that water has for absorbing and storing heat. Most of the water in the atmosphere is in the form of invisible vapour, but when the air is cooled below the temperature called the dewpoint, at which it becomes incapable of holding so much water, or when more moisture is added to it, the water condenses into drops and becomes visible as cloud.

Cloud is interesting to the seaman in a number of ways. It tells him about the state of the air mass and the processes that are going on in it and hence is his principal source of first-hand evidence about coming weather. It affects visibility when it forms in contact with the surface to produce fog or mist and when it precipitates drizzle, rain, hail, sleet or snow.

When Scratch and his mates saw the blue sky bleached by the insidious veil of cirrus they were being warned of coming events by evidence of a change in the water content of the air 5 or 6 miles above them. The formation of cloud on the land and the progressive lowering of its base was a clear demonstration, to men who lacked any kind of instrument, that the air at low levels was becoming moister and needing to be lifted less and less by its passage over the rising ground for its temperature to fall to the dewpoint. If later the cloud of the occluded warm sector had not concealed the cumulonimbus at the cold front they would have had warning of the squall, but heavy rain and hail can only come from a cloud of great vertical development and its appearance announced the arrival of a new unstable air mass whose powerful updraughts would disperse the haze of dust and water particles from the lower levels and bring a complete change of weather.

The evidence we can gather from clouds comes from their type, the height of cloudbase and cloud tops, their growth, movement and the sequence in which they follow one another.

Cloud Type

Clouds fall essentially into two basic types. Those which develop vertically and are known as cumuliform or heap-type clouds, and stratiform or layer-type clouds whose development is horizontal. Cumuliform clouds are associated with instability when temperature falls so sharply with height that rising air finds itself warmer than the air at its new level and tends to go on rising. The powerful vertical air currents produced in them make these the only type of cloud capable of generating large raindrops, hailstones and thunder. The clear atmosphere produced by the rising currents gives good visibility at the surface and a clear-cut, sharp-edged appearance to the clouds' characteristically upswelling contours.

Stratiform clouds form in air whose temperature lapses slowly with height, so that any air which has been forced upwards and consequently cooled by the reduction of pressure finds itself colder and denser than the surrounding air and tends to sink again. This produces an inversion of temperature where the air just above the cloud is warmer than that in the cloud top and acts like a lid against which the rising air spreads itself out horizontally giving the cloud tops a characteristically level appearance. The process can be repeated above the inversion to form further layers of cloud. Such clouds lack updraughts capable of supporting large water drops so any precipitation from them is in the form of light rain or drizzle. Dust and water particles trapped under the inversion become concentrated near the surface so the atmosphere lacks the clarity of unstable air and if visibility is poor it tends to remain so. A type of layer cloud called stratocumulus, which, being formed by turbulence, is especially common over the land, combines as its name suggests the characteristics of both cloud types. It is, however, essentially stratiform cloud associated with stable air, despite its rounded form which suggests rolls of dough interrupted by thin patches or even open lanes through which blue sky can be seen. These main cloud types are subdivided according to the altitude at which they occur.

Because the colder the air the less water vapour it can contain, the densest clouds occur at the lowest levels while those at great altitudes are thinner and more sparse. High clouds, made of ice crystals which give them a soft fibrous appearance and which refract light to form haloes and patches of iridescence, interest us because the weather we enjoy at the surface is largely determined by events that are taking place more than 6 miles above our heads and because clouds at that height, which in temperate latitudes move in a generally easterly direction, are visible above the horizon at a great distance.

In most circumstances high cloud gives the earliest visible indication of forthcoming change. The first thing to determine is whether it is forming or dispersing, and the easiest way to do this is to focus on an individual cloudlet at the edge of the cloud and see whether others appear around it or whether it becomes isolated or even disappears. The dispersal of high cloud is always a good sign but it does not follow that its formation is necessarily bad so we must look for further evidence from the cloud type and its movement. Mares' tails, those long curling streaks that give the sky a chaotic wind-blown appearance often form and disperse continually during fine weather when they tell us no more than we know already, that it is a fine day. When they are regularly organised, combed out into parallel rows, they indicate a sharp change of wind direction in a relatively shallow layer and that could be significant. If we can see which way the clouds themselves are moving, and which way the fall streaks are turning, we can visualise the relative wind directions and speeds at those levels. This is considerably more difficult aboard a moving boat than it is on land and opportunities for practice should not be missed. The most violent wind sheer of all has its own conspicuous advertisement in the cross-banded banner of jet-stream cirrus which traces the path of a shallow river of wind rushing at 100 or 200 knots across the sky ahead of and flowing more or less parallel with the warm front, indicating by its vigour the intensity of the parent depression. Condensation trails from jet aircraft give a clue to the state of the atmosphere according to whether they disperse in relatively dry air, persist and form cloud when the air is damper, or even trigger off the formation of a cloud sheet, but since the altitudes of different aircraft cannot be known, the evidence on its own does not justify detailed conclusions.

Clouds of medium level may serve to confirm that a frontal sequence is on its way when they succeed a previous overspreading of cirrus, and may help to fill out the bones of an over-condensed forecast by providing a clue as to whether the promised trough is frontal and if so of what kind. A non-frontal trough, lacking an uplifting slope, sends no warning sequence of clouds ahead of itself. Cumuliform clouds appearing at middle altitudes mark an intrusion of unstable air, and if their vertical development becomes conspicuous the stage is set for rapid and dramatic change. It only needs the lower levels to become destabilised, by hot sunshine on the land for instance, for the whole troposphere to become unstable from the ground upwards and break out in vigorous cumulonimbus activity and thunderstorms.

Low cloud is naturally most familiar to us, being closest and frequently obscuring medium and high cloud. Its lowest and worst manifestation is at ground or sea level when a moist wind blows across a surface cooler than the air's dewpoint to form sea fog, or when the land at night, radiating heat to space through a cloudless sky, chills the air under an inversion to create the typical land fogs of autumn. Sea fog is easily predictable if you know the sea surface temperature and the dewpoint of the air. You can avoid it if you can get into warmer water, and it is worth remembering that in some areas notorious for fogs the surface water is chilled by upwelling currents of cold water from the depths, caused by strong tidal streams encountering submarine ridges. Where sea fog is widespread it persists until the air mass is replaced, so the words of hope and salvation for the fog-bound are 'cold front'. Landsmen associate fog with light winds but at sea the two do not necessarily go together and thick fog can accompany a fresh breeze. In gales visibility is often reduced to fog levels because enough water becomes airborne to saturate the air and trigger condensation. This effect can be seen quite clearly in quiet weather when a heavy surf running on a coast forms a belt of haze greater in extent and depth than can be accounted for by flying spray.

The well-known radiation fogs of the land cannot form at sea but they can fill inlets and estuaries and drift out across coasts. If the sun shines strongly enough it usually dries them up after some initial early morning thickening, so if conditions favour radiation fog at your destination an afternoon approach should miss it. Unlike sea fogs, radiation fog is lifted from the surface and becomes low stratus if the wind exceeds 8 knots so light winds are as necessary to them as are clear night skies and sufficient moisture.

The vertical extent of cloud depends primarily on the amount of moisture in the atmosphere. The height of cloudbase, as we have already seen, gives an indication of relative humidity, while the height reached by the tops of cumulus-type clouds shows the level to which instability prevails. The dispersion of clouds, either by the lowering of tops, raising of bases or the breaking-up of cloud sheets denotes descending air, the characteristic feature of anticyclones. Air ascends in depressions, which is basically why depressions are so cloudy, but it can also be lifted by other agencies, by convection for instance, to form shower clouds and thunderstorms, or by land to make the tell-tale clouds of coasts and islands and the cloud caps of mountains. These last are often stationary, not drifting away downwind but continuously forming and dispersing at their windward and leeward boundaries. Most clouds, though, move with the wind at their own level, so by observing the movements of cloud at different levels, as well as their types and amounts, we can check on the progress of forecast developments. To do this successfully demands a modest grasp of the theory of meteorology, but all observation helps us to understand. The use of the visible evidence of the upper winds in short-term weather forecasting is ably explained by Alan Watts in his book *Instant Weather Forecasting*.

Wind

The seaman's interest in the wind is threefold. Wind provides his propulsive power, is the major influence on the state of the sea and hence the strains on his crew, hull and rig, and is a valuable indicator of the progress of weather systems. The study of meteorology shows us how air is set in motion in response to differences in pressure or temperature, and how that motion is influenced from the moment of its birth by the combined effects of the earth's gravity and rotation, but it stops a little short of representing the actual physical force of wind so the mental picture is at odds with reality. The reason for this goes back a little in recent history.

The Beaufort Scale

During the early years of the nineteenth century Admiral Sir Francis Beaufort specified a scale of wind strengths in thirteen steps ranging from Calm, *force 0*, to Hurricane, *force 12*, which were described by the conditions prevailing on board a large man-of-war of the period. Many countries adopted this scale and when the anemometer came into use suggestions were made for a precise standard description in terms of wind speed. International agreement was eventually reached in 1926 and the Beaufort Scale was standardised with each Beaufort number corresponding to an exact range of wind speed. Five more divisions, taking in speeds up to 118 knots, have since been added.

If you are an aviator you are interested in the speed of the wind because together with its direction it forms an essential vector in determining your drift and enabling you to navigate; but if you are a wave

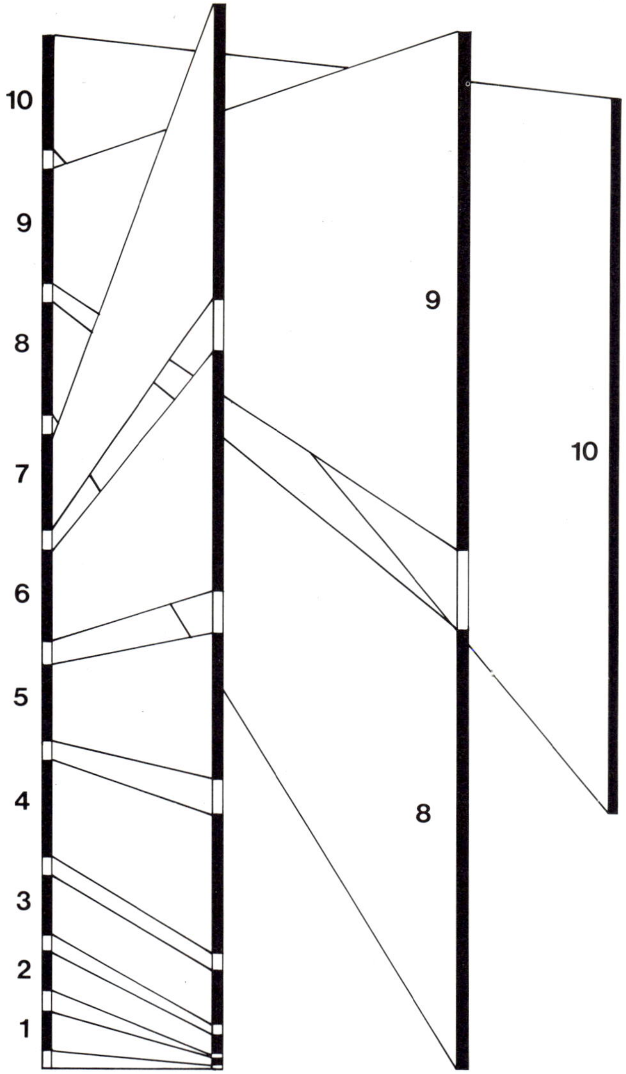

Fig 2 Part of the Beaufort Scale: on the left it is divided in proportion to wind speed. The three right-hand columns show the corresponding changes of pressure

or a sail, or a woman wearing a wide-brimmed hat, or a man trying to consult a map, what is affecting you is not the speed of the wind but its pressure, which varies not directly with the speed but as its square, so that doubling the speed quadruples the pressure, trebling the speed causes a ninefold increase and so on. Of course this makes no difference in theory, and even in practice the mind makes the necessary adjustment once it has become familiar with the relationship but, though there are good reasons for calibrating the Beaufort Scale in speeds rather than in pressures, it does make it harder to appreciate its proper significance.

When we think of the Beaufort Scale in terms of wind speed we form a picture of roughly even divisions, with the wind's force increasing steadily over the scale with the speed but, as the diagram (Fig 2) shows, the intervals become quite different when the scale is redrawn in terms of pressures. One of the most interesting features of this diagram is the lengthening of the gaps in the scale, which illustrate the increase of pressure corresponding to a 1 knot increase of wind speed at different parts of the scale. This is conveniently shown by the curious omission of a knot between each division.

A minor consequence of thinking of wind force in terms of speed is that we tend to overestimate strong winds. Life begins to get pretty grisly in a small boat when the wind reaches force 6 and, when it has got considerably worse with a 58 per cent increase in pressure stirring the cauldron of the sea and demanding a major sail reduction, we are unwilling to believe that it has not yet reached at least force 7, even if there is an anemometer to tell us.

Forecasts often give a range of wind strengths without saying that the wind will freshen or moderate from one to the other, but meaning that the wind will either fluctuate over this range, or that it will vary from one part of the area to another. Which it is can only be decided by your knowledge of meteorology and ability to use other evidence, but its significance is obscured if you use the scale of speeds rather than pressures, as you can see if you consider '4 to 6' or '5 to 7', which occur quite frequently in the forecasts. Similarly, when the forecast speaks of '6 gusting to 8', it could mean a 25 knot wind gusting to 35, which is 1·4 times the speed but double the pressure.

Apparent Wind

A change of heading or the turn of the tide can have a pronounced effect on apparent wind, so we seem to experience a freshening of the breeze as the tide begins to run to windward; and just as everything goes mercifully quiet when we bear away and bring the wind aft at the end of a breathless beat, we all sooner or later experience the unpleasant surprise of coming on the wind after a fast downhill run and discovering that we are horribly over-canvassed. You would think that changes of apparent wind would be more dramatic in light winds than in strong ones, because the change of speed is proportionately so much greater, but this is not borne out by experience,

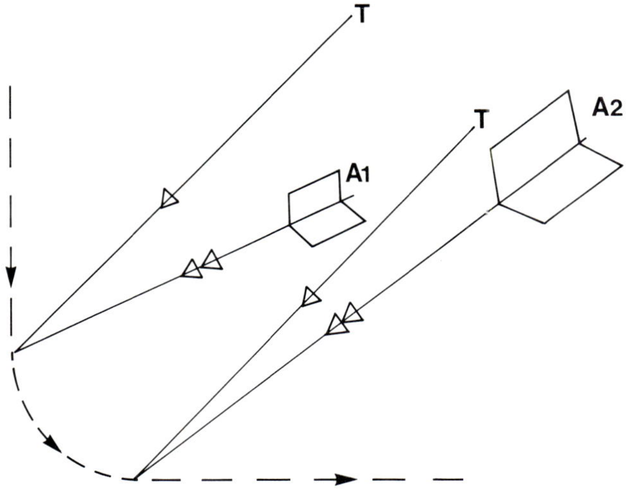

Fig 3 The effect on the apparent wind of rounding up from a broad reach to a fetch: *T* is the true wind of 20 knots; *A*1 is the apparent wind when reaching at $7\frac{1}{2}$ knots; *A*2 is the apparent wind when close-hauled at 5 knots. Wind speeds are represented by the overall lengths of the lines. Wind pressures are proportional to the areas of the arrow tails

and the reason can be seen if we look at the diagram of the Beaufort Scale in terms of pressures, which shows that for a given change of speed the pressure change at force 6 is three times what it would be at force 3.

When a boat is broad reaching at $7\frac{1}{2}$ knots with a true wind of 20 knots 45° on her quarter, she feels an apparent wind of $15\frac{1}{2}$ knots 24° abaft the beam (Fig 3). If she hauls her wind until she is close hauled at 45° to the true wind and making 5 knots over the ground, the apparent wind becomes 24 knots 37° on the bow. The apparent wind has increased from force 4 to 6 and the pressure has more than doubled.

Squalls

Not to be confused with gusts, which are irregular fluctuations of the wind caused mainly by interference with its free flow, squalls are sudden increases in the wind strength, often accompanied by a change of direction, which last for several minutes and die away equally suddenly. They occur when fast-moving air from aloft is brought down to the surface by the vertical currents of an unstable air mass, and the greater the height to which instability extends, the greater is the likelihood and severity of the squalls.

The signs by which we can anticipate squalls are the height to which cumulus and cumulonimbus cloud extend, and if the cloud tops are not visible this can be judged by the weight of precipitation. If a real shower of rain or hail is falling, the cloud is a cumulonimbus, the vertical currents in its vicinity are powerful, and the massive downdraught of air entrained by the falling rain can be expected to produce an outrushing squall at the surface. Such clouds occur at cold fronts, in maritime polar air and in thunderstorms. The squalls associated with a cold front are known as line squalls from the line of dark cloud, appearing to an observer at the surface as an arch, which precedes them, and are accompanied by a sudden wind shift and fall in temperature.

It has to be remembered that cloud and precipitation owe their existence to moisture in the atmosphere and if the air is dry a line squall, for instance, can exist without any visible sign other than the evidence of wind at the surface. Fortunately perhaps, this situation is scarcely possible at sea in temperate latitudes, but the air may be dry enough for the base of a cumulonimbus cloud to be as high as 2 or even 3 kilometres and for precipitation reaching the surface from it to be light or non-existent, so the absence of low cloud or an active shower cannot be read as signs that a squall does not exist.

Since thunderstorms develop in fully mature cumulonimbus clouds, any thunderstorm is a potential source of squalls. Although they can happen at any time of the year, some of the most violent occur near the continental coasts of Europe in summer, an area which includes south and east Britain, when shallow lows form over the Continent and drift north. The pressure gradient round these lows is typically slack and surface winds so light that they may be masked altogether by draughts from the clouds' convective activity. The unwary and the forgetful may be unpleasantly reminded that the severity of the squall depends on what is going on at the top of the cloud and is not related to the deceptive calm at the surface.

When the air is so dry that there is too little cloud evidence, or so moist that there is too much for it to be visible, the only warning of a squall's approach may be the whitecaps it raises on the sea and the behaviour of other craft in its vicinity. This may leave little time for shortening sail, so it behoves the mariner to keep his weather eye cocked.

Coastal Winds

The winds that are useful to the sailor fall within a relatively narrow range of strengths at the lower end of the Beaufort Scale. Force 2 is too light for progress except in smooth water; the upper end of force 5 is strong enough to dull the keen edge of pleasure in turning to windward, while force 6 has long been recognised as 'the yachtsman's gale', sheer misery for all but experienced well-organised crews in well-found, well-managed boats. As we have already seen, the effects of sea and tide can be equivalent to a couple of notches on the Beaufort Scale, so local or temporary variations in the wind can be of critical interest.

The wind of basic meteorological theory, air set in motion by pressure gradients, obedient to Buys Ballot's law, retaining the innate characteristics of its source region and bearing the imprint of its subsequent wanderings, corresponds pretty closely to the winds actually experienced over the open ocean. The presence of land, however, exerts powerful, widespread and complicated influences which would take a whole book to explain properly, and coastal winds tend to differ in speed and direction both from those of the open sea and those inland.

Land and sea breezes caused by the unequal heating and cooling of land and sea by day and by night are perhaps the best known manifestations of coastal winds. These thermal winds are important to the mariner because of their power to change the wind near the coast and make it radically different to that experienced out at sea. Understanding them can make the difference between finding a working breeze or lying becalmed, enjoying a favourable slant or having to beat, sleeping tranquilly in a quiet anchorage or having to turn out in the small hours and put to sea. They deserve studying in depth and I shall say no more about them here than to urge attention to the influence exerted by the form and aspect of the land. This can be illustrated by the following account of the formation of an extremely local thermal wind in Skye, which was caused entirely by the surrounding topography.

Land and sea breezes do not develop widely on Scotland's west coast because the high latitude and the steeply westward-sloping coast combine to delay the period of maximum heating by the sun until late in the day and reduce its intensity. So sea breezes tend to be confined to the sea lochs and those that do develop on the open coasts start late and are usually weak. Conversely the late lingering sunlight and short nights reduce nocturnal cooling and make land breezes rare. On this occasion a faint sea breeze on the quarter had carried us south through the Inner Sound, and at early evening left us becalmed off Kyleakin. Lochalsh stretched ahead as smooth as a sheet of glass, ringed with sunlit hills under a cloudless sky. We had unquestionably had our ration for the day, and in order to save our tide through the narrows of Kyle Rhea we stowed the sails and motored. Kyle Rhea is a narrow gorge from which the heights of Knoydart and Skye rise steeply to east and west, forming a funnel through which the wind as a rule pours, like the tide, along its length regardless of the true wind direction, but on this calm evening a smart breeze was whipping across it from west to east, ruffling the surface right from the water's edge at the weather shore. This wind was caused by the western shore being in shadow, while the eastern was still warmed by the sun. Air, cooled by contact with the shadowed mountainside, was flowing down from a height of 700 metres, crossing the Kyle and becoming a convective current up the Knoydart shore.

Where land features cause wind streams to converge, the local wind strength may be greatly increased. This can happen when wind deflected along a steep coast joins air funnelling out of a valley, or in a bay where valleys converge. Conversely, an area from which wind diverges, such as the centre of a large bight across whose shores the sea breeze is blowing, is likely to experience light winds or even calm. It would be very convenient if we could make a distinction between those features that tend to increase the wind and those that exert a diminishing influence but so much depends on the air itself, its temperature, humidity and stability, and so much on the land itself that the picture easily becomes woolly and indeterminate.

The first feature to strike us about land is that it affords shelter. Not only does it cut that most important consequence of wind, sea, by restricting the fetch, but it actually reduces the speed of the wind itself. It does this because the friction of its uneven surface absorbs the wind's energy and retards its lower layers, slowing them down so much that the speed of an onshore wind is commonly cut by a half within a few miles of crossing the coast and may even be reduced by a factor of five. In his excellent study of thermal winds, *Wind Pilot*, Alan Watts gives the useful rule of thumb that wind strengths reported by land stations should be doubled in order to obtain the probable wind over the open sea. The lowering of wind speed causes its direction to be deflected less by the Coriolis effect, so the amount that the wind is backed (in the northern hemisphere) relative to the isobars is about twice as much over land as over sea.

Friction is most effective at night when turbulence is least. By day the turbulence created by surface heating of the land continually re-energises the surface layers by linking them with the faster-moving air aloft, thus we have the familiar experience of the wind inland dying down at nightfall and springing up again shortly after sunrise. When a light or moderate wind blows across a narrow piece of land, such as an island or peninsula, it sometimes happens that daytime turbulence, extended upwards perhaps by a rugged terrain, causes the wind by day to be stronger in the lee of the land than on its windward side. At night the more normal situation is restored and the lee side becomes sheltered.

The vertical extent and steepness of land has an important bearing on how it affects local winds, but the outcome depends so much on the characteristics of the air mass that it is not possible to give any simple rules. The best that can be done is to consider the factors involved and the possible consequences of their interaction.

Wind prefers to flow round rather than over an obstruction and what it does depends on both the length and height of the obstacle. Funnelling occurs when the flow of air or any fluid is restricted as it is in flowing round a wing or a sail, past a headland or through a strait. Its effect is to accelerate the air in the region of restriction and is regularly encountered wherever there are mountains, islands and headlands, as well as in actual funnel-shaped features like valleys and straits. The higher and steeper the obstacle, the greater its effect on the wind, and many major headlands have bad reputations for local winds which are further enhanced in many cases by strong tidal streams.

The lee of mountains seldom provide good shelter, and very often such places are highly unpleasant in gales because of the fierce squalls that sweep down from the heights. Sometimes a mountainous island like Madeira is narrow enough to part the airflow as a boulder parts a stream, so that there is a wide 'wind shadow' of near calm with land and sea breezes along the coast in its lee while the prevailing wind funnels round its ends. But if the mountain barrier is long enough to dam the airflow and force some of it to climb over the top, a variety of things can happen. Sometimes a system of standing waves is set up, their crests usually marked by conspicuous lens-shaped clouds some distance to leeward of the mountain ridge and their troughs marked by areas of increased winds which frequently drift slowly so that at a given place near-calm and winds of force 6 or 7 succeed one another every few hours, the wind taking only a few minutes to reach full strength or to die away. As the air in the lee of the mountains is usually dry, the weather is apt to be fine and the lenticular clouds, which do not drift downwind because they are continuously condensing and dispersing in the crests of the standing waves, are useful warning signs. When cold air is dammed up behind a mountain range, it can spill over suddenly and, because of its high density, rush down the leeward slopes with great ferocity, spreading gale-force winds far out to sea. Certain parts of the world are notorious for these effects, which are given local names, but they can occur anywhere even on a small scale when the conditions are right, so if there are mountains to windward, look out for squalls and be specially wary if a vigorous cold front is approaching them from the other side.

Forecasts usually make allowance for these effects, when they occur on a large enough scale, as for instance the funnelling of north-east winds in the Straits of Dover or off Cape Finisterre and of north-westerlies off the Naze of Norway, but they also occur quite frequently at other places on a scale much too small for notice in the forecast: the mariner has to make his own prediction by recognising the circumstances that can produce them.

5
The People

5

Before a vessel can do anything beyond embellishing her harbour, someone must have the urge to take her to sea. People must assemble and embark. Their belongings, food, water, fuel and the host of items needed to enable them to carry out their intentions must be put aboard and stowed. Someone must make the decision to go and must communicate it to the rest. Sails and running gear must be prepared, the anchor weighed or mooring slipped. Once under way her course must be directed, her progress verified and she must be handled in such a way as to exploit the natural forces that both propel and oppose her. Throughout, both she and her company need to be maintained in a proper state of fitness to their purpose. The efficiency with which all this is done is the measure of a crew's seamanship and until this measure is taken the seaworthiness of the vessel is as open a question as the athleticism of a foetus.

What are the crew's tasks? What demands do they make? How can the demands be eased and the crew's ability to meet them be increased?

These are questions for the whole crew, not just the skipper, for by considering them everyone can gain a better insight into the functioning of the ship and his own part in it.

The Crew

Whether a boat is manned by one man or by many makes little difference to the fundamental tasks which have to be done. The single-hander has to do everything himself. He assesses his own ability, makes his own decisions, carries them out himself with a minimum of fuss and misunderstanding. Given sufficient physical and moral stamina his task is relatively simple; he knows no problems of communication; congratulation and recrimination weigh on him no more than do dead leaves; his decisions for the most part commit no one but himself. His hardest task is to ensure his own fitness to achieve his aim and fulfil his obligations to other seafarers.

Increasing the number of the crew enables the work to be broken down into lighter individual burdens, allows more time for rest and recreation but introduces the need for communication and co-ordination, and since the decision-maker no longer acts for himself alone, multiplies the burden of his responsibility.

The professional seaman enjoys the advantages of an established organisation in which members of a crew are appointed to perform the various tasks, and a recognised standard of manning appropriate to the type of ship and the nature of her operations. But, except in the case of a keen racer, the amateur crew is seldom recruited primarily for reasons of seagoing efficiency; more often the process is almost haphazard. Boats of similar size and type can be found crewed by a single individual, a family party, a group of friends, or a crowd of youngsters with one or two experienced adults. One crew may consist entirely of seasoned experts; another may contain one person capable of doing everything while the rest can do nothing without close supervision; a third may be composed of beginners under the command of the most articulate or the most self-confident. However diverse these crews may be, however dissimilar their competence and their intentions, they all share the same fundamental need for decision. As decisions often have to be made quickly, one man must be responsible for making them, and the first post that must be filled is that of decision-maker or skipper, and the second, since we are all mortal, is his understudy. As the skipper's function is more clearly perceived in relation to that of the rest of the crew we will leave him to the last and start by considering the other positions that have to be filled.

In the war galleys of the ancient Greeks, movement about the ship was hampered by their great length and the presence of banked benches of oarsmen, so the division of duties was partly territorial. The 'bow officer' was responsible for the activities that went on forward—such as lookout, anchoring and beaching—while aft the 'steersman' was responsible for navigating, directing the quartermasters and handling the ship. In our day it is more usual to make functional divisions and I have not yet heard of a multihull crew reverting to territorial responsibilities.

Here then is a basic division of duties aboard a vessel that puts to sea for the sake of the voyage. A single-hander has to perform them all himself, but the members of a small crew may each combine two or more duties, while in a large crew they can be further subdivided to spread the responsibility and the experience and so promote individual talent. The titles are unimportant and can be replaced by numbers or whatever you like: it is the responsibilities that matter.

The Mate

As the skipper's deputy and second-in-command he needs to be competent to take over at any moment. Traditionally responsible for domestic organisation and the day-to-day running of the ship, he makes out and supervises the watchkeeping roster and sees that the necessary but boring household chores are equitably divided among the crew. A good mate creates a foundation of unobtrusive orderliness (never to be confused with 'bull') on which the crew can operate efficiently and eliminates sources of minor friction between individuals that so easily undermine the harmony of a crew.

The job calls for a temperament that is exactly the reverse of the rip-roaring ready-fisted heroes of salt-horse fiction. It needs observation, the ability to listen, sensitivity to other people's mental and emotional states, tact, firmness and a sense of humour. Small-boat life often entails overcrowding, fatigue, anxiety, motion sickness and other stresses which render normally tolerant people curiously raw-nerved about minor irritations. You find yourself at one moment readily forgiving the man who steps on your face, and the next wanting to strangle him for some harmless mannerism. One of the most common causes of disharmony is a member of a crew giving the impression that he is taking advantage, taking more and giving less than the others: if he monopolises the best space, avoids the worst jobs or is late turning out for his watch, a debilitating tension develops which lowers individual efficiency and destroys crew unity. Of course, those who think themselves injured can defuse the occasion by refraining from resentment but just try it: under the circumstances it demands heroic virtue, but a good mate can anticipate and prevent the situation from arising.

Sailing Master
The term is self-explanatory and the office is a useful means of delegating an important and interesting job.

Steward
This title is used in preference to 'cook' since there may be many cooks taking their turn at this important chore, but one person must be in control of the acquisition, handling and stowage of provisions and the maintenance of galley equipment. He should keep the skipper informed of any matter that may affect his decisions such as an anticipated need to replenish. Not a satisfying job for most people,

The unexciting chores. . . .

should be combined with something rewarding. . . .

and a share of deckwork and steering

and an arduous one if combined with cooking, so in a small crew, when roles can be doubled, the steward's other hat should be something rewarding, such as bosun or navigator, and in a large one the mate should make sure that he is allowed a fair share of deckwork and steering.

Bosun

Responsible for the condition of all the yacht's deck gear, her standing and running rigging, sails and spars, ground tackle, mooring lines and so on. Besides being handy with a marline spike and sail needle he needs a sharp eye to spot incipient deterioration, and determination to get on with the job when he may be tempted to procrastinate. If a ship has a good bosun, gear failures are rare; if she has a very good one all her crew become competent marline-spike seamen as he passes his skills on to them. Where the crew contains children, parts of the job can be delegated to bosun's mates with responsibility for such specific items as the dinghy and its equipment.

Navigator

As with catering, regardless of how many people take part in navigating the ship, there needs to be one person in overall charge to coordinate their work, be responsible for all equipment, and see that all necessary books and charts are available and corrected up to date.

The raw material with which a navigator works is evidence. There is seldom enough of it and usually the more it is needed the more scanty it is. Sometimes this cannot be helped, but more often the reason for the shortage is because crew members are unaware of the need, and ignorant of the means of obtaining and recording it. Some navigators behave as if the ability to navigate depended on a wonderful occult power which they alone possess, and discourage all attempts to penetrate the simple logic of their craft, with the result that they deny themselves the co-operation and assistance that few in their circumstances can afford to be without. Every member of the crew should be encouraged to navigate and, while it is not advisable to let more than one person on each watch do the actual plotting, there are often opportunities for 'prentice hands to have a go under supervision and so learn to appreciate the problems. Everyone on board should be capable of taking bearings, timing lights, estimating the moment when an object is dipping, and recording navigational evidence in the deck log book.

Engineer

In most auxiliary yachts this is rather too grand a title for a position involving no engineering skill, but it is more accurate than 'mechanic'. The engineer is responsible for the operation and maintenance of all mechanical and electrical equipment and associated spares and tools, and for the provision of fuels and lubricants. He instructs other members of the crew in the correct use of equipment and ensures that standard procedures such as the starting and shutting down of engines are followed. As his field of responsibility overlaps somewhat with that of the bosun, the line must be carefully drawn to ensure that such things as winches, pumps and fire extinguishers do not get left out and that each knows who is responsible for what. Depending on age and ability, a child could profitably do the whole job or assist as 'second', if possible having distinct areas of sole responsibility.

General Duties

In a small ship's company most, if not all, must be chiefs and every chief an Indian. Before we start looking at the function of the skipper, let us consider the basic skills which every man should attain before he can consider himself a seaman.

Communication: Rather obviously he must be able to understand orders and instructions and make himself understood, so he needs a working knowledge of nautical terminology. Some people object to what they see as a semi-secret code designed to create a mystique and help an exclusive clique of initiates to feel superior. But the plain fact is that nautical jargon is plainer than 'plain English' because it does the job it has to do more explicitly and concisely, and considering the looseness with which we habitually express ourselves anyway, with remarkably few ambiguities. If anyone doubts this, try translating a few phrases or ponder the confusion latent in the substitution of 'right' for 'starboard'.

Communication between members of a crew goes a long way beyond the mere understanding and obeying of orders; there must also be a feedback of information. This is needed to confirm that the order has been correctly understood, and to acquaint whoever is controlling the operation with its progress so that he can correctly judge the co-ordination and timing of other actions forming part of the same evolution. A crew member should always acknowledge an order by repeating enough of it to indicate that he has heard it correctly but there is no need to repeat the whole order word for word. Professional seamen do this automatically and the habit distinguishes them immediately in an amateur crew. The helmsman being relieved tells his relief to steer one five eight. 'One five eight', repeats the relief, and eliminates the possibility that the navigator will appear on deck some time later to discover that the ship's heading has become one nine eight. Unfortunately the results of neglecting this simple precaution are not seared as indelibly into the memories of crewmen as they are into those of skippers and it can be an uphill struggle to gain co-operation in this respect.

Comparatively few of the operations involved in the management of a boat are observable in their entirety from the cockpit and the bigger the boat the more difficult it is to see what is happening on the foredeck or down below. Even if we take the simplest possible situation, such as getting underway from a swinging mooring, the need for the feedback of information is of obvious importance. Everything is ready. The skipper orders 'Let go.' The foredeck hand acknowledges, casts off and reports 'All gone.' Sails are trimmed and the boat is under command. If the foredeck hand fails to report when the boat is free of her mooring the skipper must either ask him, await the indications of the boat's behaviour, or take a chance that his order has been carried out. The first two alternatives involve delay, the third risks the gamut of unpleasant consequences ensuing from the boat gathering way while fast to her mooring: all could wreck his plans.

One hand for the ship and one for yourself: Everyone who goes to sea owes certain duties to his shipmates and to other seafarers that he can only discharge by looking after himself. The inexperienced but enthusiastic sometimes affect indifference to fatigue and discomfort, allowing themselves to get soaked and cold, and remaining on deck for hours in the mistaken belief that they are demonstrating keenness and hardihood. However deeply and genuinely a man may love the sea he must remember that he no longer has the gills that he sported for a brief period of his embryonic life, that he is utterly and irrevocably dependent on the land, and that the sea is for him a hostile and potentially lethal environment in which he can only hope to survive by avoiding or protecting himself from its effects.

The good seaman recognises that his first duty to his mates is to take care that he does not fall overboard or get hurt and to keep himself as far as possible warm, dry and free from seasickness and fatigue, and that the second is to see that his personal gear is always in good condition and properly stowed. The extent to which he succeeds in these tasks determines not only how much of his own talent can be effectively used in the service of his ship but how little the efforts of others need be diverted on his behalf.

Basic skills: The basic skills of a crew member are summarised in the Practical Course Syllabus for the RYA Competent Crew Certificate. Although the official course may be run and course completion certificates issued only by authorised instructors of RYA, recognised teaching establishments, skippers and watch leaders who are themselves competent ought to be capable of coaching less experienced members of their crews to this level. As part of their responsibility to their crews is to educate, this syllabus is the logical indicator of the standard to which they should aspire. With permission of the Royal Yachting Association, I reproduce this syllabus in full from RYA publication G15/78, Cruising Proficiency (Sail) Syllabus and Logbook and Certificates of Competence.

A QUALIFYING EXPERIENCE: has been an active crew member for five days on board a sailing vessel in commission, including 100 miles at sea in tidal waters, and four hours' night watchkeeping.

B ALL CANDIDATES:

1 *Knowledge of sea terms and parts of a boat, her rigging and sails.* Sufficient knowledge to understand orders given concerning the sailing and day to day running of the boat.

2 *Sail handling.* Bending on, setting, reefing and handling of sails. Use of sheets and halyards and their associated winches.

3 *Ropework.* Handling ropes, including coiling, stowing, securing to cleats and single and double bollards. Handling warps. Ability to tie the following knots and to know their correct use: Figure of eight, Clove hitch, Rolling hitch, Bowline, Round turn and two half hitches, Single and double Sheet Bend and Reef knot.

4 *Fire precautions and fighting.* Awareness of the hazards of fire and the precautions necessary to prevent fire. Knows action to be taken in event of fire.

5 *Personal safety equipment.* Understands and complies with rules for the wearing of safety harnesses, life-jackets and personal buoyancy aids.

6 *Man overboard.* Knows action for recovering a man overboard.

7 *Distress signals.* Can operate distress flares and knows on what occasions distress flares should be used.

8 *Manners and customs.* Understands the ordinary practice of seamen and yachtsmen with regard to: Use of burgees and ensigns, Prevention of unnecessary noise or disturbance in harbour including courtesies to other craft berthed alongside.

9 *Rules of the road.* Is able to keep an efficient lookout at sea.

10 *Dinghies.* Understands and complies with the loading rules. Is able to handle a dinghy under oars or engine.

11 *Meteorology.* Is aware of forecasting services and has a knowledge of the Beaufort Scale.

12 *Seasickness.* Working efficiency unaffected/partially affected /severely affected by seasickness.

C SAIL TRAINING CANDIDATES ONLY:

13 *Helmsmanship and sailing.* Is able to steer a compass course and understands helm orders. Understands the trimming of sails to windward, reaching and running.

14 *Logs.* Is able to read a log.

15 *General duties.* Has carried out general duties satisfactorily on deck and below decks, in connection with the daily routine of the vessel.

D YACHTING CANDIDATES ONLY:

16 *Helmsmanship and sailing.* Understands the theory of sailing and can steer and trim sails on all points of sailing. Can steer a compass course, under sail and power.

17 *Engines.* Is able to start, stop and carry out simple checks on inboard or outboard engine.

E DESIRABLE BUT NOT ESSENTIAL ITEMS: The following items are desirable, but not essential. Items (19) and (20) are mandatory for the award of the Day Skipper/Watch Leader Certificate.

18 *Personal survival.* Holds ASA award for personal survival or is able to swim 50 yards in light clothing.

19 *Artificial resuscitation.* Has been taught and fully understands the mouth to mouth method of artificial resuscitation.

20 *First aid.* Knows the contents of the first aid kit and is proficient in emergency first aid.

The Skipper

The master of a vessel has overall responsibility for her and her crew and, although he does not need to be as expert as his subordinates in their individual skills, his knowledge and understanding must be very thorough if he is to support this responsibility.

His job is to make decisions and carry them out through the management of his ship/crew combination. Just like any other member of the crew, the skipper must protect his own fitness to do his job, being particularly careful to see that he gets enough rest because he above all others must avoid the disabling effects of fatigue. What the crew lacks in numbers or expertise the skipper may have to supply in his own person, performing the functions of some or even all of the 'heads of departments' and being general dogsbody as well, but this puts him at the disadvantage of being pulled this way and that by conflicting priorities, and the more he can delegate the better he can concentrate on his primary function of making decisions.

What happens when a skipper has too many claims on his attention can be seen by looking at a perfectly ordinary situation.

A yacht in which the skipper, perhaps for good reasons, does practically everything himself is on passage down channel, bound towards Dartmouth from the Solent, which she left early that morning on the first of the fair tide. It is now early afternoon and she is close-reaching to a southerly breeze about 4 miles SE of the Shambles. If things remain as they are she should reach her destination at dawn, by which time according to the morning forecast a warm front could be beginning to affect the Plymouth area. This has placed the skipper in something of a dilemma, for he is nervous about being caught in Lyme Bay by a rising onshore wind and deteriorating visibility, yet reluctant to divert to the shelter of Weymouth because he knows that in the veering winds behind the trough his not very weatherly vessel may be stuck for days awaiting a chance to get round Portland Bill when she could be cruising under a weather shore in Devon. In order to make up his mind he needs up-to-date intelligence on the movement of the front and so it is important to him to hear the 1355 shipping forecast. If he delays his decision until the next forecast at 1750 he will be west of Portland, with the west-going stream running at full strength, and therefore badly placed if he hears that the trough has speeded up and he does decide to go back to Weymouth.

Five minutes before the forecast he sees that all is well in the great outdoors, that the helmsman is happy, tunes the radio and prepares to take down the forecast, muttering impatiently at the leaden witticisms with which the disc jockey pads out the allotted period of his programme.

At last the forecast begins, and as his pencil is poised to take the synopsis there comes a shout from on deck.

'Skipper!'

A fishing boat, previously thought to be no threat, has altered course the way fishing boats do and has faced the helmsman with a situation he does not know how to handle.

'Skipper!'

Cursing, the skipper turns up the volume and gets to his feet, shakes the man dozing on the settee, asks him to get the forecast and goes on deck.

They miss the forecast. The offwatch member of the crew has not had enough practice at taking it down, misses most of it and can recall next to nothing of what he has heard. The skipper is too preoccupied in avoiding the fishing boat to take it in, even though he has turned up the volume and tried to keep his ear cocked.

The essence of this situation, that of a man having to be in two places at the same time, can be brought about in scores of different ways, most of them like this example in quite ordinary and not extreme circumstances. The immediate danger, which our skipper avoided, is that a man faced with conflicting priorities tends to choose the one that was originally on top. It is not at all unusual for a man in this position, intent on a vital task to dismiss all other claims, even those of emergencies: in fact it sometimes seems that an emergency serves only to lock the attention all the more irrevocably on to the wrong object.

No one can be considered a competent skipper if his wits are not nimble enough to switch priorities when necessary, and the one in our example clearly passed this test, though there are plenty of people in charge of boats who could not do so, and no one should ever put himself in a situation in which he becomes so engrossed in secondary aims that he loses sight of his main objective. Had our skipper been less on the ball—possibly because of tiredness or seasickness—he might either have failed to respond to the helmsman's call, acted too slowly, or misjudged his subsequent actions, all with serious results. As it was, he came through with nothing worse than the failure to get the forecast which he so much needed for the furtherance of his primary aim and so, being a cautious man, he decided against going on and spent two days needlessly windbound in Weymouth.

It would clearly be absurd for a skipper to avoid doing any of the practical work of the ship, but if ever he finds himself having to do something because no one else can do it properly he has identified a target for improvement.

Inexperienced skippers often try to take too much on themselves, but just like anyone else in the crew the skipper has a duty to maintain his own fitness, to husband his strength against the time when a tired crew will look to him for clear-headed leadership, and the wise man takes life easily when he has the chance, knowing that the sea will soon enough give him the chance to show what he is made of.

Make yourself redundant: I suspect that one reason why many of us go to sea for 'pleasure' is quite simply to fulfil a basic urge to stand on our own feet. For an increasing number of people, life on shore frustrates this urge. Many of a man's actions are pre-ordained by regulation, by precedent, or the plain lack of an acceptable alternative. If he does get the length of making a decision he is apt to find it overruled because it does not agree with the policy of some remote 'body', or is made ineffective by the chain of events stemming from some obscure dispute between unknown people on the other side of the world. Even those in positions of high responsibility complain when announcing a 'decision' that they 'have no alternative . . .'. At sea there are still, by and large, a number of alternatives open in most situations. The problems are essentially straightforward. The factors affecting them are comprehensible to anyone prepared to go to a little trouble, and a man's decisions are free from arbitrary modification by other people, however much we may protest that we have only to decide to go west for the wind to blow from that quarter. If the sea cuts a man down to size it also gives him substance, 'These are counsellors', said the exiled duke, 'that feelingly persuade me what *I am.*' So everyone who has made port in good order after a hard passage must have felt the faintly intoxicating sense of his own reality that persists for the few moments that it takes for humility to evaporate and topple it into the entirely different sensation of pride. No wonder skippers are tempted to hog the stage and run the whole show.

But only the single-hander can afford to indulge his awareness of self-dependence; the skipper with a crew has to imagine himself dead or at least incapable, and the measure of his true calibre as a skipper will be reflected in his crew's ability to manage without him.

The idea of a skipper being relieved of his command by *force majeure* is not in the least far-fetched, it can happen to any of us. And when it does someone needs to know or to have access to the facts that will enable him to discover the present position of the boat and the action needed to bring her and her people safely into harbour. If the navigational plot and the contents of the last forecast are in the skipper's head, and he has fractured his skull in a fall or has succumbed to a heart attack, someone among the shocked and bewildered survivors is going to need to be more, not less, competent than he was.

It would seem self-evident that if a skipper trains his crew to a level at which they can manage without him he will not only improve the chances of his own survival if he should fall overboard or meet with any other mishap, but the overall seaworthiness of his ship will also be greatly improved. Yet how many skippers and crews really pursue this aim?

I once knew a couple, intelligent professional people, who lived for their summer cruise. He was an expert seaman, keen and full of ideas. She loved the life, enthused about the experience but beyond taking the helm took no interest in the practicalities. 'I leave all that to my husband. He's the expert.' One day he fell overboard and they both lost their lives.

Crew Organisation

To illustrate the division of responsibility, here is a summary of the individual tasks that would need to be done in preparing a yacht for sea.

1 *Skipper*
- Crew fit and briefed for the intended passage.
- Passage planning completed.
- Official papers in order and any courtesies or obligations appropriate to the nationality of the port discharged.
- When appropriate, inform neighbours of intending departure.

2 *Mate*
- Crew's personal lockers and bunks allotted.
- Watchkeeping roster published.
- Below-deck stowage complete.
- First aid and medical stores checked.

3 *Steward*
- Enough fresh water. FW system working.
- Food stores complete. Identification and location organised.
- Cooking equipment and tools checked and stowed.
- Cooks briefed.

4 *Bosun*
- Sails fit for use and correctly stowed.
- Repair gear checked.
- Rigging set up. Chafing gear complete.
- Ground tackle, mooring warps and fenders serviceable and all not in use stowed for sea.
- Spares and tools checked.
- Deck-stowed emergency equipment checked for condition and security.
- Yacht's tender and its equipment securely stowed.

5 *Navigator*
– Appropriate charts and books up to date and stowed.
– Plotting instruments complete.
– Compasses serviceable and deviation cards displayed.
– Navigation instruments (sextant, chronometer, barometer, log, etc) checked and uncorrected errors recorded.
– Radio equipment and spare batteries checked.
– Navigational plan prepared.

6 *Engineer*
– Sufficient fuels and lubricants for engine, cooking and heating.
– Portable containers for liquids securely stowed.
– Batteries charged and all electrical systems working.
– Spare bulbs and fuses correctly marked and stowed.
– Engine serviced and ready for use. Crew instructed in starting and stopping routines.
– Spare parts and tools complete and stowed.
– Bilges dry and pumps tested.
– WCs working properly, spares checked.
– Seacocks free and set as required.
– Condition and stowage of all emergency equipment not carried on deck. (e.g. fire extinguishers)

7 *All hands*
– Understand safety precautions and emergency drills including abandoning ship, action in the event of fire, man-overboard procedure, use of distress signals.
– Safety harnesses properly adjusted.
– Foul-weather gear in good repair.
– Personal possessions properly stowed.

6
Teamwork

6

The bunch of individuals assembled in the confined space of a boat does not automatically become an efficient crew just because everyone knows his job and understands the mutual responsibilities that embrace them. They have to be able to work together smoothly like the parts of a machine which, if they are not truly adjusted as to fit and clearance, dissipate energy through friction and damage one another. Communication, which has already been mentioned, is a vital first step, for no progress can be made until it has been established, but it becomes less and less evident as a crew matures and in one whose members are well used to working together it may seem to the onlooker, if it is discernible at all, to have entered the realm of telepathy.

Given long enough practice, a crew will eventually reach this happy state of being able to work in a co-ordinated manner without any apparent governance, but the process can be speeded up and the awkward period of adolescence reduced if internal relationships and organisation are studied.

Aims

The first essential when creating a crew is that everyone should understand both the purpose of his own actions and the object of the operation in which he is taking part. If he does not, he can hardly be expected to feel the same interest in, or responsibility for, his efforts and, even if he carries out his orders in minute detail, the result is liable to disappoint expectation. He himself will be disappointed because he feels he has not been given a fair chance and his skipper will feel, correctly but unjustly, that the man has not given of his best.

A skipper must therefore make his own intentions clear to the crew: this can be a valuable exercise for him since it involves his first discovering what his intentions really are. An unfamiliar evolution may need quite a thorough briefing but this can be abbreviated as the crew gain experience until a word or two is enough to convey the intention. Thus the skipper on the first day of a training cruise might have to say, 'We shall be going alongside, almost certainly outside another boat, port side to. To begin with we shall want one line forward and another aft. If there is no one to take them, one of us will have to go aboard when we get alongside and the forward line will have to be secured first. We shall also want fenders rigged to port with one loose on the cabin top, amidships.' After the operation has been accomplished successfully a couple of times he can convey his intention simply by saying 'Going alongside. Port side to.'

Orders

Next he must give his orders. Regardless of the crew's experience or the degree of informality in the manner in which they are communicated, orders exist to supply three essential pieces of information. *Who* is to act, *what* is to be done, and *when* it is to be done.

1 *Who is to act*: If the person who is to carry out the order is not named, the skipper's intention is likely to be thwarted in a number of ways:

(i) No one does anything because everyone thinks someone else will do it.
(ii) Several people leap to their feet and collide, or rush off to the far end of the boat where they become so engrossed that no one hears the next order.
(iii) Someone who is already engaged in another task abandons it so as to attend to the new order.

The first two possibilities can be eliminated if individuals are assigned to the job. The third is a bigger problem, being a form of

CRANFIELD SAILS

indiscipline to which some people seem specially prone, but as long as a skipper gives broadcast orders he cannot begin to extirpate it because he is in no position to insist that the culprit sticks to the job he has been given. Such a person has to be given a responsibility that keeps him physically close to the skipper and relatively inactive so that he can see what the rest of the crew are doing and learn to trust them to work without his help. Too many people on a job get in each other's way and spare hands hovering on the edge have a way of becoming so riveted that their attention cannot be deflected on to what they really ought to be doing.

2 *What is to be done*: The aim here must be to convey the whole of the intention precisely without unnecessary words. These words must be well chosen and the shades of meaning of expressions such as 'ease out', 'pay out', 'let fly' and so on understood. Vagueness and ambiguity in an order are to be avoided both for the obvious reasons and also because their existence probably betrays vague and ambiguous thinking. A preliminary briefing which brings everyone into the overall picture helps the person who is going to give the orders to organise his own thoughts, and by priming his hearers to keep those orders brief.

3 *When it is to be done*: Many operations take their cue from other events. For example, when the mate of a watch decides to rectify a sagging headsail luff next time the boat is put about, he may say, 'Bill, will you sweat up the jib halyard when she comes head to wind.' Bill then goes forward and gets ready to act without further orders.

On another occasion there may be a need for a 'stand by' order so that the job can be done at a moment which will be judged by the person giving the order, rather than by the one who executes it. It enables all preparations to be made for instant action, but requires a

(*Opposite*)
Too many hands. The foreground figure is a beginner being shown a practice sail-change

'go' signal, which may be a word, a gesture, or even a whistle.

Use of Voice

It is a waste of effort to take care over choosing the words you use so that they convey your meaning exactly, if you then allow the tone in which they are delivered to give them a meaning that is entirely different, so the use of the voice needs as much care as the words of the order. It can be difficult to get the volume right. Shouting is best avoided. No one likes being shouted at and noise in any form raises the general tension, but it is sometimes necessary to compete against all the racket a boat can make in a strong wind and a rough sea and then you need good lungs and projection. Once again good preparation makes fewer words necessary and, in daylight at least, visual signals are useful.

The power of the voice to affect the emotions is an important factor in an emergency. A man so tired that he seems totally unresponsive and 'out on his feet' can be restored to full vigour instantly if you can anger or frighten him enough. A good shot of adrenalin flooding into the bloodstream is unsurpassed in its capacity to banish extreme fatigue, but the methods used to provoke it lose their potency as soon as the subject gets used to them. 'Loud-mouthed swine. He's always like this when it gets dirty' thinks his brain as it turns over and goes to sleep again, and his glands never even get started.

Initiative

When a crew has settled down together, its members reach an instinctive ability to recognise how much rein they can give their own initiative and judgement. This is very noticeable to a newcomer to a crew, who is likely to be under some stress until he feels himself in tune in this respect, for he can sour his relationship equally by going too far as not far enough.

The problem is one that ought to be considered by every member of the crew, though it is the skipper who has to take the lead and make his attitude plain, because if it is not tackled it will be the cause of endless misunderstandings and detract heavily from the crew's efficiency. The question is: does the skipper, or his deputy, expect to initiate every operation himself or only those major ones which affect the overall progress of the passage, and if this is so, at what point does he draw the line? There are some skippers who stamp relentlessly on any sign of initiative and many of these have been wrenched into this attitude by the direst experiences. I believe the best they can hope for from their crews is that they will eventually become useful passengers, able to do exactly as they are told and to co-ordinate their efforts with reasonable success, but I do not believe that they can ever bring them either to the pitch of efficiency or to the level of enjoyment which they are capable of attaining. Under certain circumstances such as Sail (meaning character) Training, dude sailing, and short-term adventure activities, there is virtually no alternative because the crew barely have time to learn enough to be able to take in what is happening, let alone recognise the need for some kind of action and know what to do about it, so if someone gets a rush of genius to the head and does what he believes to be the right thing without reference to anyone else the possibilities for disaster are huge.

When a crew sail together regularly, however, most skippers would grumble if he heard the sails slatting and found the helmsman staring fixedly at the compass, unaware that the wind had headed, or if he found that no one had bothered to take bearings of an approaching ship. But what about minor adjustments to sails or the rig? A good crewman in an unfamiliar boat, doubtful about how much initiative is expected of him, will tactfully volunteer to perform some action which seems to him necessary and will gradually build up a frame of reference to guide him. Difficulties arise if he seems to be prompting the skipper to do something which he intends to do anyway but for which the time is not yet ripe, and one who is bashful about appearing ignorant or who has received a blast of withering scorn for speaking out of turn or stating the obvious may resolve to keep his mouth shut in future.

Raising the Standard

When the members of a crew understand their intentions the next step is to extend their understanding to their actions by physical practice. Ideally a crew ought to carry out every operation it is ever likely to perform before it can consider itself fit to set out on a passage but, as with many ideals, practical obstacles get in the way and we end up with a compromise.

The regular manoeuvres like sail drills that can be carried out without interrupting a passage present no problem. It is easy enough to set in turn every sail the ship has, including storm sails, or to rig and use the emergency steering gear so as to make sure that all the necessary equipment is in working order, that the crew knows where it is stowed and how it all goes together. Provided these sort of exercises can be completed on the first day, and the gear is known to be free of defects that cannot be repaired at sea, there is no need to delay the start of a passage until they have been done. Unless the start is made late in the day, working the crew all together for a few hours before regular watchkeeping is begun can help everyone to settle down.

More complicated and disrupting exercises, like Abandoning Ship, Man Overboard, or Fire, call for different treatment because real live rehearsal involves unacceptable risk and cost, and too sketchy a simulation is misleadingly unrealistic. Nevertheless the advantages of physically going through the motions are so great that we must simulate where necessary and recognise the limitations and artificiality of what we are doing.

The trouble with a live liferaft launch is that it renders the liferaft useless until it has been repacked, and if we leave this job until the end of the season, not only is this the wrong time for the effectiveness of the exercise but inflating and wetting the liferaft results in an enormous increase to the cost of the annual servicing. One answer is to

(*Opposite*) A practice sail-change: organising the lowered sail for bagging and . . .

spread the cost by organising a joint practice for as many individuals as possible. This suggests a swimming-pool event at the end of winter, when a larger number of people can watch the inflation and undergo the experience of righting and boarding the raft than would be possible at sea, even in unrealistically mild conditions. A practice like this gives no idea of the behaviour of a liferaft alongside a sinking yacht in a gale of wind but its value can be increased if it is controlled by someone who has used one in earnest.

The man overboard emergency rightly receives a lot of attention and would continue to do so even if we could guarantee that no one would ever fall in, for no other situation combines so many different elements into such a perfect lesson for instructors, or such an illuminating occasion for examiners. It demands preparedness, overall comprehension, sense of priority, judgement, resourcefulness, decision, crew management, skilful boat handling and deckwork. By the same token, it makes an admirable crew exercise with almost endless scope for variation, but since practice with a live victim is virtually ruled out by the elaborate precautions that would be needed against loss of contact or prolonged immersion, it is again important to make sure that everyone understands the difference between the exercise and the real thing.

Every operation contributes towards crew training in two distinct ways: through the experience itself and through the opportunity it makes for analysis and discussion, and both should be used to the full. At the end of the exercise everyone concerned should consider what went right or wrong and what might be altered to improve the result, and at the first convenient opportunity the various views should be compared. If a real shambles occurs, it may be necessary to take the whole thing apart in a detailed post mortem, but for the most part it should be enough to deal quite briefly with essential points. Getting it right is the most essential point but an inexperienced crew may not realise what they have achieved if no one tells them.

(*Opposite*) bagging it

Training sessions can be great fun and crews enjoy them when they are intelligently directed. To get the best results they should be organised as games in which a variety of operations follow one another in succession, and there is here an apparently undeveloped opportunity for club events that test aspects of seamanship competitively on the lines of the Combined Training events and Mounted Games of riding and pony clubs.

Unless a crew is already very good and keen to reach an impeccable standard, it is best to avoid numerous consecutive repetitions of the same exercise. If the first attempt is a mess, identify the faults and try again. The second shot is likely to be much better and may justify a third but, unless the crew are encouraged by their own success to want to go on and do better, it is best to change to another exercise at this point. Whenever repetition fails to show any improvement change the subject; people can only take in so much at a time and it is vital for an instructor to recognise and respect the signs of saturation. Animal trainers know that the fruits of much effort can be wasted by pushing a lesson too far: human teachers need no less to be able to judge when to stop.

(*Opposite*) Training sessions can be fun

7
Physical Well-being

7

A crew can operate effectively and with enjoyment for as long as it continues to find interest in its activity, maintains a balance between its output and intake of energy and gets enough rest. There is an evident link between physical health and mental enjoyment. A person who is feeling off colour is typically listless and generally finds it hard to take an interest in anything outside himself, while one who is bored or fed up falls an easy prey to ailments including seasickness.

Eating and Drinking on Passage

Doing physical work and keeping warm, expend energy at rates which vary greatly from the easy life of a downhill passage in warm weather to short tacking in a fresh breeze when the work is hard enough to make you quite warm, even in a cold climate. Maintaining body temperature while just sitting about in the cold and wet can deplete energy as quickly as hard physical work. To replace lost energy we need food, in sufficient quantity and frequency, and water, both for the conversion process and to replace that lost through sweating, increased breathing during exertion, and evaporation by wind and sun.

On shore we fall into habitual eating routines which depend mainly on local custom, and the human body accustoms itself fairly easily to almost any pattern, but basically eating and drinking is confined to the active half of the day, meals or snacks being spaced out at roughly four-hourly intervals between 0800 and 2000, while little or nothing is taken in the remaining twelve-hour period, of which about two-thirds is spent in sleep. When we miss a meal on shore, the body sets up a mild protest at about the time when the expected meal fails to materialise, producing symptoms that may include faintness, headache and nausea, as well as the familiar sensation of hunger. After an hour or so, however, these symptoms disappear in a healthy individual until his inner clock alerts his system to be ready for the next expected meal. At sea, hunger symptoms are often accompanied by a feeling of cold and can easily develop into seasickness, so that instead of being geared up to eat like the man on shore, the digestive system of the hungry mariner prepares itself to reject the food which he so much needs. If he is sick, this increases his energy deficiency together with his reluctance to do anything about it, makes him feel terrible and starts to deplete his water content which increases his suffering and eventually endangers him if it is allowed to continue.

Once this vicious circle has become established, it is difficult to break so we must prevent hunger symptoms from appearing by keeping our fuel and water topped up. At sea, the digestive system needs to be lightly loaded at frequent intervals and it is better to take numerous light meals round the clock, rather than the more widely spaced relatively heavy meals with the long night fast that are customary on shore. To satisfy the habitual rhythms of the body and prevent it from raising false alarms, eating needs to be organised so that some of these snacks occur at conventional meal times. Since this type of eating largely displaces so-called 'proper' meals, it is important to consider variety and balance of diet. Trying to live on biscuits and chocolate and cups of tea is no use at all and will quickly produce an ardent longing for steak and kidney with two veg, for which no one will have much appetite when he actually gets it. The aim should be not to increase the number of conventional snacks but to space out the ingredients and quantities of conventional meals.

This approach solves other problems as well. One of the main difficulties in cooking in a small vessel at sea is that of controlling large numbers of pots and utensils. Even in a well-arranged galley, preparing a two- or three-course meal can be a punishing task that leaves the cook hot, out of temper and very likely seasick, but eating little and often means that, although the total quantity of food prepared and consumed is the same, the amount to be coped with at any one time is less and the task simplified. The more unconventional pattern of eating also allows much more flexibility in watchkeeping routines. Conventional meals have to coincide with the changes of watch and usually the relieving watch eats first and those coming off make a second sitting with yet more problems for the cook: if a three-watch system is used the meal will occur in the middle of one watch's off-duty period and there may be a dilemma as to whether they should be roused in order to eat or allowed to sleep on and perhaps be very hungry by the time the next meal is due.

Many people find the early morning a trying time: dirty weather is even more depressing when you can see what you are going through and, even if a beautiful dawn elevates the spirit, the wizened features of those figures hunched in the cockpit assure you that, like yours, their eyes feel like dead cinders and their tongues like dead mice. Part of the trouble is caused by trying to go to sea with shore-based eating habits. Watchkeepers need more than biscuits and sweets to keep them going through the night. At midnight they should have a hot drink with cheese, fruit or maybe even a hot-dog or bacon sandwich, and at four o'clock a first instalment of breakfast: a tummy full of hot porridge makes a splendid sleeping draught for those turning in and puts some heart into those going on watch in the chill of dawn.

Within the limits imposed by the difficulties of storing fresh food diet should be as varied as possible: a monotonous diet is unlikely to be balanced and interest is as essential to successful eating as it is to any other activity. The type and quantity of food varies with climate as much as with individual preference. In the snow on top of a mountain you can wolf stuff that would turn you up if you met it in warm sunshine several thousand feet lower down. It is the same at sea. The high-energy foods so welcome in high latitudes attract little interest when you are looking for ways to keep cool, though raw fruit and salads are welcome in any climate.

Seasickness

Sooner or later almost everyone succumbs to this demoralising complaint and there is no use in pretending it is all in the mind or that chewing melon seeds or anything else confers immunity, because whatever you say about it, or whatever you think has been proved in one case, is disproved by the next or contradicted by someone else's experience.

The best defences against seasickness are reasonable physical fitness—which includes being free from a load of old *haute cuisine* and *premier cru* when you go to sea and keeping warm and properly nourished when you get there—a quiet mind and acclimatisation. Being in good condition is an obvious advantage, so is absence of anxiety, since the associated tensions can make you sick even on dry land, and there is some crumb of comfort to be had in the depth of affliction from the knowledge that sea time confers a degree of immunity on almost everybody.

Many people are helped by the various drugs that are available but it is essential to use them properly and to know how you personally react to them. So far as I know no drug is effective if its use is delayed until the symptoms of seasickness are felt and none can be guaranteed free of side effects for every individual. The most common side effect is drowsiness, which may render a person more dangerously incapable than if he were seasick. Sometimes this can be minimised if treatment is begun the evening before sailing, when the first dose knocks you out cold and after a night's sleep the effect of subsequent doses may be less severe. Having watched people dose themselves regularly for days on end on long passages I suspect that an attempt should be made at weaning after forty-eight hours, by which time many people have begun to find their sea legs and relative immunity. Those who persist with the drugs seem to become mentally peculiar but perhaps they would seem that way anyway after four or five days at sea.

Experienced members of a crew can often detect the first signs of impending seasickness in others before the victims themselves are aware of it. The demeanour becomes listless and depressed, the loquacious fall silent, bright eyes become dull as interest in the external world wanes, consciousness turns inward, skin colour changes and posture becomes hunched or slumped. If the victim is below decks he will feel a need for fresh air, if on deck he may feel cold. He will be disinclined to make any effort and going below for an extra sweater may be the last straw, but keeping warm is important so someone should get the sweater for him and encourage him to put it on. He needs active occupation but must avoid strenuous exertion or violent movements, especially of the head, so let him take the helm and not refuse the plain dry biscuits that you then hand round. All this must be done in such a way as to avoid suggesting to the sufferer that you think he is going to be seasick.

When a person has succumbed and paid tribute he may with luck feel a lot better, at least for a time, and this in itself will stiffen his resolve not to give up. For anyone seriously affected, however, the only cure is rest in a warm bunk with as much stillness of the head as possible. As long as vomiting continues, the chief danger is dehydration and the sufferer should be encouraged to sip cold water.

Rest

Fatigue is the arch enemy of the sailor. It transforms able men into dolts, makes them see and hear things that are not there and fail to see what is in front of their eyes. A tired man cannot perform simple calculation, decision and judgement elude him, impressions reaching his brain baffle him because he cannot interpret them. I believe that the high accident rate among trawlermen, compared with men doing comparable tasks with similar equipment in merchant ships and ashore, is largely attributable to lack of sleep while they are on the fishing grounds.

The effects of fatigue appear in two stages. In the first the victim feels and looks tired and his brain and limbs slow down but, given enough determination, he can keep going with surprising vigour and may even forget that he is tired until either the need for continued action ceases or he reaches the second stage. The significant difference in the second stage is that, although determination may continue to keep him on his feet, it cannot keep his brain working properly and stop it playing tricks on him. One of the first things to go wrong is co-ordination of hand and eye so that the victim misjudges manoeuvres which he is normally capable of performaing accurately. Errors creep into simple calculations and go undetected. When tables have to be consulted, he lifts figures from the wrong column or even the wrong page. Later the victim finds himself bewildered by objects that he cannot recognise—a pattern of lights that would normally indicate the type and heading of another vessel becomes unrecognisable or is wrongly interpreted. Eventually he may start to hallucinate when his brain registers real visual images of non-existent objects and events.

While the outward signs of what I have called the first stage of fatigue are physical, those of the second stage are emotional: the subject laughs or cries for slight reason and is unusually irritable. A group of people may for no apparent reason infect one another with helpless laughter or a normally placid person become suddenly irascible. These symptoms bring their own problems but above all they signal the need for action to counter an imminent and drastic fall in efficiency through fatigue.

Watchkeeping systems exist to make it possible for every member of a crew to be fit and alert during his hours of duty, and every crew that goes to sea for more than a few hours needs to have a scheme of watchkeeping ready to put into effect if the outing looks like being prolonged to more than eight hours. When passage-making, watches should be set as soon as possible after sailing and on no account should this be left until evening or the whole crew will begin to feel tired at the same time.

The kind of system adopted depends on many factors and can be varied to an almost unlimited extent to take account of the specific needs of the crew and the prevailing circumstances. The first question that has to be settled is how many people are available for watchkeeping and how many are competent watch leaders. Suppose, for example, the crew consists of skipper and four others, of whom two are capable of taking charge. This allows of two watches of two men without involving the skipper, which is clearly a promising start since his responsibilities make it desirable for him to be excluded from watchkeeping if possible.

The next point to be decided is the length of watches. This will depend on the strength of the crew, the weather and the demands of the boat. Two reasonably fit adults should be able to share the traditional four hours' watch in good summer weather in a suitable boat, but if the weather is cold or inclement, if the crew includes the very old or very young, the boat is difficult to steer, needs frequent sail changes, or habitually throws water all over the cockpit the period may have to be reduced. If the crew can manage three-hour watches by night, they can probably do four-hour ones in the daytime, but except for the few people able to cat-nap, four hours is about the minimum time that will allow them to get a long enough rest before going on watch again. In this case, one way of extending sleeping time would be for the skipper to stand one or two watches by himself. For every watch the skipper does, both regular watches get a double period below. Thus if watches are relieved every three hours at 0100, 0400, 0700 and so on, and if Starboard is on from 0100 to 0400, Port from 0400 to 0700 and the skipper takes over from 0700 to 1000, Starboard is off from 0400 to 1000 and Port from 0700 until Starboard come off at 1300. This gives all the watchkeepers an opportunity for at least five hours' uninterrupted sleep in each twenty-four hour period without imposing an unacceptable burden on the skipper.

When there are enough competent watch leaders, a three-watch system can be used. This gives everyone two watches off for each one on, which makes three hours an admirable length for watches. As the skipper is likely to be on permanent standby anyway, the three-watch system can often be operated with watches of only one person. In crews so small that the skipper has to stand regular watches it may be possible to extend the period of continuous rest by making daytime watches very much longer. A crew of two might relieve one another every three hours during the night but each do a watch of six hours during daylight.

While it is vitally important to have enough sleep, 'enough' is less than many people imagine. Five or six hours a night is not bad going and even sleeplessness is nothing to worry about, provided you can lie relaxed and warm. In these conditions we may believe ourselves to be completely wakeful while in fact getting a surprising amount of sleep in fitful dozing. It seems to be the skipper's fate to have to turn in all standing because he usually has to be ready for the deck at a moment's notice, but it is much more restful and refreshing to change into pyjamas and go to bed properly, and those who suffer from cramp after three or four hours in a cold cockpit are recommended to turn in wearing a dry pair of wool socks.

Some thought has to be given to the times at which watches are relieved. There is bound to be a fair amount of disturbance at the change of watches and it is obviously convenient to arrange eating to coincide, but the receiving of weather forecasts and some navigational activities occurring at fairly fixed times are made more difficult if the entire crew is counter-marching across the unfortunate who is trying to do them, so the watch change should be kept clear of these events.

The practice favoured by competitors in short-handed long distance races, of having an overlap period when both crew members are on watch together, could be more widely used. It has the advantage of affording some valuable social contact, an opportunity to discuss tactics and to undertake tasks that need all hands without encroaching on anyone's precious time-off, or bringing about a situation in which one watch is indebted to the other. It also disposes of the question of whether the duty cook is provided by the watch on deck or the watch below.

Security

No workman can do a decent job unless he has a solid support for himself and his work. The navigator cannot plot, nor the cook cook if they have to hold themselves and their implements against the accelerations of the boat. All hands are exposed to injury from falling or from the gear and to the risk of going overboard if they lose their grip or balance at a critical moment. Even rest becomes impossible if you have to brace yourself against being rolled around in your bunk so physical security is one of the primary requirements of life at sea, just as proper stowage is the basis of material seamanship.

Precise two-handed movements, such as those that cooks and navigator have to use, are only possible when the body is securely held in the region of its centre of gravity which lies roughly between the hips. This is most satisfactorily provided by a snug seat with low sides, but if space is too restricted, horizontal rails or webbing slings can usually be contrived to support the user in working position without the need for him to use his hands to hold on.

Both on deck and below skid-resistant surfaces are essential underfoot, while handholds are needed in strategic positions to facilitate movement about the vessel. Vertical pillars are more useful than horizontal grab rails because an arm can be passed round a pillar and the body anchored, while the use of both hands is still retained, but there is an obvious limit to the number of pillars and these should be sited where they will be most useful. Bare teak is an excellent surface, wet or dry, and allows a stable sitting position for deckwork in rough weather but gelcoat and oilskin make a hopelessly slippery contact, even when the gelcoat is textured to give a non-skid surface. Those on glassfibre decks must rely on the grip provided by the soles of their shoes, and any areas of deck that need it should be given extra treatment to afford a better grip.

Crews should be encouraged to get into the habit of moving about, both on deck and below, using their hands as well as feet like monkeys, even in fine weather, and going from one handhold to the next.

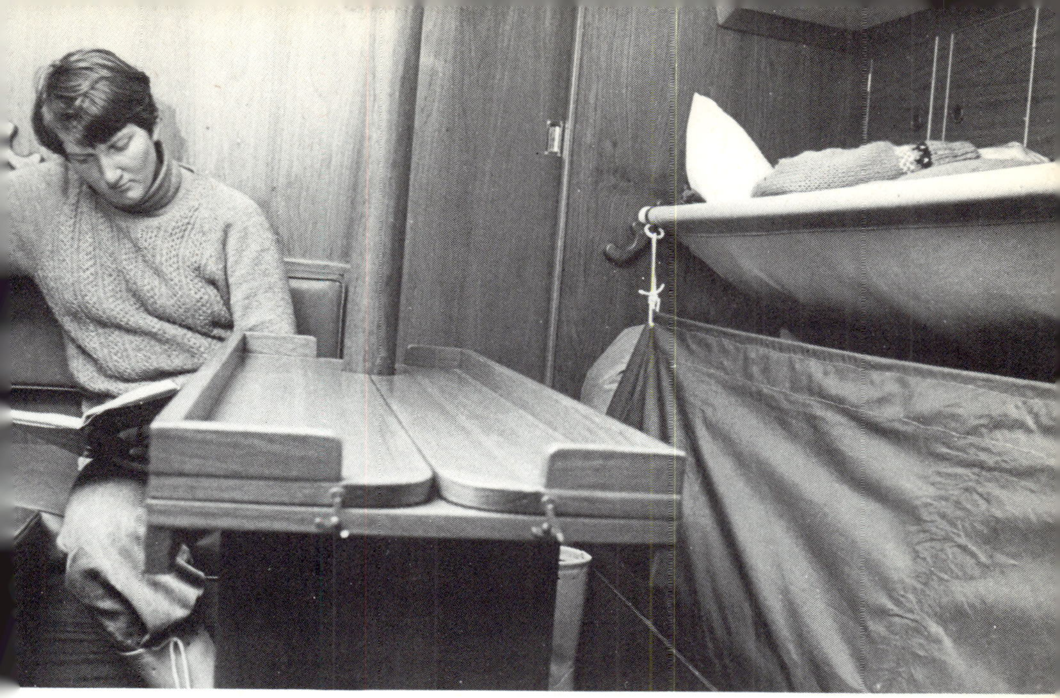

(*above*) Physical security for the watch below is essential for proper relaxation

(*below left*) Getting ready for the deck, using handholds

(*below right*) Foot- and handhold. Note galley safety strap in foreground

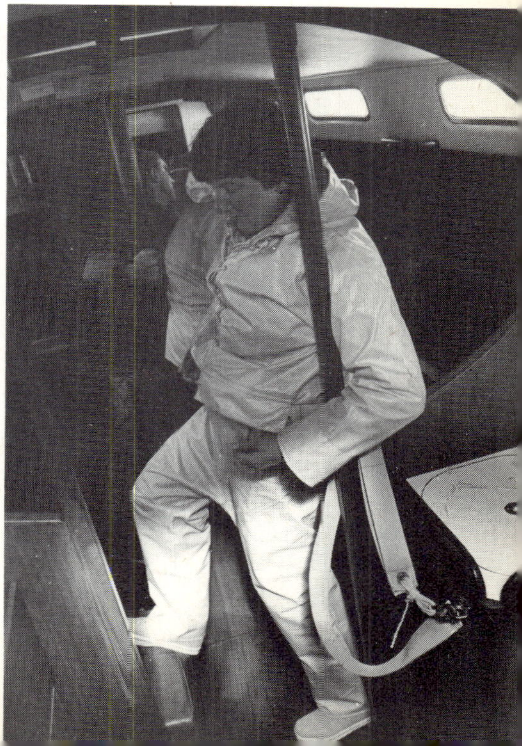

In this way people's hands soon learn where all the holds are and seek them automatically. Harnesses are heavy and uncomfortable and their lifelines exasperatingly incommoding, yet they should always be worn when the motion is violent, and at night. Harness should also be worn when anchored in a tideway if there is any sea and no dinghy in the water astern of the yacht.

A final thought to be chewed over by male members of the crew, as they lean gracefully out over the lee side with an arm encircling a shroud while groping among four inches of insulation for the vital plumbing, is that in the Roman navy *urinator* was the title of a diver.

8
Stowage

8

Just as crewmen need to be able to remain securely in position while they work or rest, so they need to be able to find any needed item of equipment fit for use in its expected place without having to ask questions or turn out lockers in a search. However chillingly sterile we may find immaculate order on land it is a basic necessity for working at sea that everything should have its own place, recognised by all, from which it departs neither by accident nor intention except when it is in use and to which it returns when that use is done. No job is finished until all tools and equipment have been returned to their stowages.

Good stowage is essentially organisation for action. It is as dynamic an operation as the bowler's run before he delivers the ball and has nothing in common with mere tidiness which can cripple vital action if it is allowed to subordinate operational readiness to a neat appearance. The first step is to create the right attitude by ensuring that everyone has a place for his own personal gear because only then is it reasonable to insist that everything should be in its rightful place and not left lying about or parked wherever anyone thinks fit.

Given the amount of gear that has to be carried on any seagoing vessel, the lack of space in all but the largest yachts, limitations of size, weight, vulnerability and accessibility imposed by many of the spaces available for stowage, successful results demand clear thinking and a rigorous sense of priority. The requirements of each item have to be weighed against the limitations of the vessel. These are:

Weight: Heavy weights need to be disposed low down, amidships, and kept out of the ends of the hull.
Protection: The whole of the decks, cockpit, cockpit lockers and bilge spaces are a submarine environment and anything stowed there is liable to be submerged or at least take heavy splashes. A good deal of

Order is a basic necessity for working at sea

water is also apt to be distributed round parts of the accommodation adjacent to hatches and places where wet people or sails come below. Flues and exhaust pipes may be hot enough to melt sails and rope in contact with them and cause damage in other ways.

Security: Changes of angle of heel and accelerations because of the motion of the sea cause things to move unless they fit the stowage or are restrained by packing or lashings.

Accessibility: Not all stowages are easy to reach under all conditions. For instance, top access to spaces under bunks is obstructed if someone is asleep in the bunk, and a gimballed cooker may swing across a locker door on one tack. In general, the most accessible stowages are also the most exposed to sea and weather.

Magnetic interference: Ideally the vicinity of the compass should be kept clear of all materials capable of distorting the earth's magnetic

The stowage plan has to allow for the occasional inaccessibility of lockers like this one

field, and though it is possible to measure and compensate for the effect of fixed objects this cannot be done for portable items which must therefore be excluded from the area. Six feet can generally be regarded as a safe distance but, when checking whether an object is affecting the compass, it must be remembered that the effect alters with change of heading and other factors, so a margin must be allowed beyond the apparent minimum safe distance.

The stowage requirements of some items are so stringent that they limit choice to very few locations. Containers of gas and volatile fuels, for instance, have to be stowed in ventilated spaces from which leaks cannot reach the bilges and are thus restricted to the deck or cockpit. This can conflict with the requirement to keep magnetic material away from the compass and in turn demand that the object which will normally remain stowed when at sea is always sited in the same place and attitude so that its effect remains constant.

The biggest and heaviest item carried in any yacht is probably a rigid tender for which there may be no option but to go where it will fit. A deflatable on the other hand makes few demands and can be stowed in a wide variety of positions depending on what is left after other things with more stringent needs have been accommodated. Spare anchors and lengths of chain being heavy and impervious to wet are obvious candidates for the lowest bilge spaces.

All spare and bulk material for which the need is foreseeable and not imminent can go into spaces of limited accessibility. This would include bulk food—from which a ready-use locker is replenished at times when access to the bulk store is convenient—rope, canvas, paint and any replacements which have to await the completion of preliminary work before they can be brought into use. Again weight and low need for accessibility point to low-level stowage for anything that can withstand damp or be given additional protection. Tins, being made of thin steel plate, corrode quickly and are often highly magnetised during manufacture so they need to be kept clear of bilge water and compasses: if they are to be stowed for more than a few weeks remove paper labels and mark contents indelibly on the tin.

A high need for accessibility brings fierce competition. Emergency equipment may be carried around for years without ever being used at all, yet it must be instantly accessible all the time and must not be allowed to gravitate to the bottom of a heap of stuff that is in frequent use. A marina-based boat going out for an afternoon sail will need her mooring lines and fenders again in three or four hours, and though it may be tedious to stow them right at the back of a locker from which other things have to be removed before they can be broken out again, this may be the right place for them because the need for them is foreseeable and there will be plenty of time to do it.

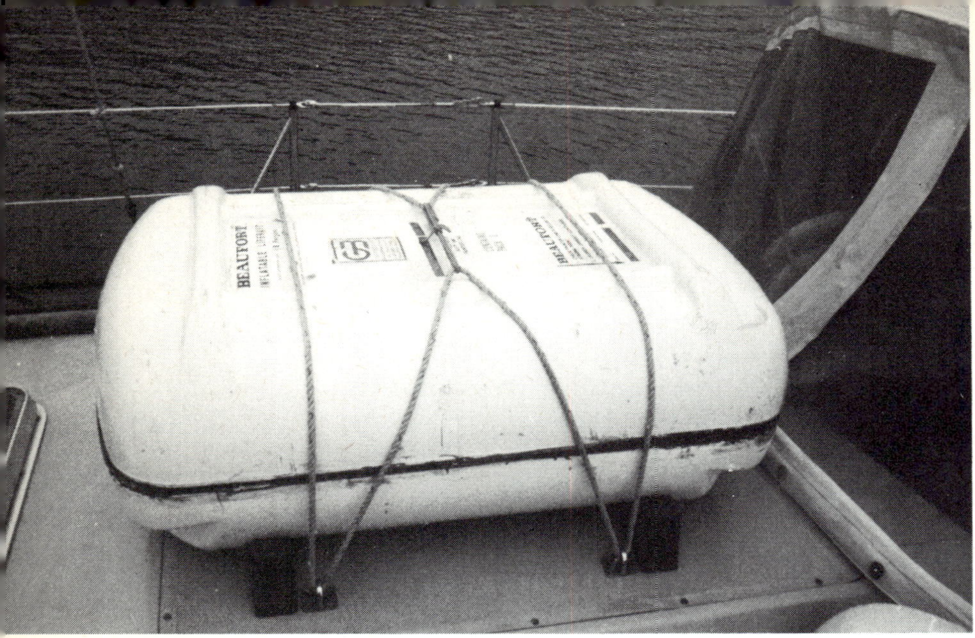

Example of good lashing: the rope is continuous, forming four bights, two of which are strained together by a few turns of a lanyard, itself secured by a simple quick release hitch. All the parts do useful work, stretch is kept to a minimum, adjustment is positive and easy, and release is virtually instantaneous under any conditions

Example of bad lashing: a continuous rope lashing consisting of a multiplicity of turns, some of which contribute nothing to the security of the load. Taking up the slack resulting from the stretch inherent in this arrangement would be a laborious business for two people, and an axe would be needed to free the liferaft in an emergency

To relieve this pressure of competition for limited space that is easy of access, it helps to split things up. Obviously all fire extinguishers need to be instantly available, ideally from on deck though this is rarely possible, but distress signals and steamer-scaring white flares are needed only one at a time: if one or two are immediately accessible—perhaps secured to the inside face of a locker door or lid—the rest can be got out while the first is being discharged. In this way, enough for instant use can be stowed really close to the action while the others can be kept together in a waterproof pack in better protection and still ready for movement to wherever they may be needed—such as into a liferaft. The same principle, which is really only an extension of the practice of carrying a shackle key in your pocket, instead of keeping it in the tool box, can be widely applied. The box marked 'Electrical Spares' can be relegated to a stowage of low accessibility if a few key items such as spare fuses and certain bulbs are removed from it and taped to convenient surfaces at the places where they will be needed.

Lashings

Everything that is stowed on deck, and some things below, need to be positively secured. This is most conveniently done by a rope lashing which, whether quasi-permanent or requiring to be cast off quickly, needs to be adjusted from time to time because rope stretches and no lashing can do its job unless it is kept tight.

A good lashing is simple, every part of it does useful work, minimises the opportunity for stretch, and is easily adjusted and cast off. The most common faults are caused by using a long length of rope which is secured at one end and then rove back and forth so that it has to be worked round turn by turn in tightening and the whole length hauled out when casting off, and by making useless turns that serve no purpose except to increase stretch and make adjustment more difficult.

The longer the line, the further it can stretch, so long lashings

Fig 4 The lanyard in photograph on page 122

have to be made of line that is heavy enough to resist stretching, but it is usually possible to arrange a separate adjusting part with several turns of lighter stuff that is easier to adjust and, incidentally, to cut in an emergency. This exactly reproduces the mechanism of a shroud set up by a lanyard: the main length of rigging is heavy to resist stretch, while the lighter lanyard is handy and its several parts provide purchase for easy straining. A long continuous line can be used if it is arranged in bights which converge over the load without actually encircling it. The apexes of the bights can then be strained together by a circular lashing of light line, which when cast off allows the bights to be pushed clear and the load to be released without the need to unreeve the main lashing.

9
Handling Rope

9

The way a man handles ropes and lines tells you more in a short time about his competence as a seaman than any other single thing, and no seamanlike skill has so much influence on the success or failure of an operation. Many a well-thought-out, skilfully executed manoeuvre has degenerated into a shambles because of a snarled-up line, and many a potential disaster has been averted by one adroitly handled.

The essential problem with rope is to gather it together into a manageable bundle from which it can be rapidly run out without becoming snarled up. There are many ways in which a rope can be organised so that it is convenient for handling and stowage, but few that ensure that it does not form kinks as it straightens out, because it is the kinks which pick up and scatter turns in disorder, and kinks which jam in fairleads and the swallows of sheaves.

The conventional way with spirally laid rope is to coil it in the direction of the lay, which is almost invariably right-handed or clockwise. Coiling against the lay is so disastrous that it is sensible to insist that all lines, whether laid or braided, should be coiled clockwise, a healthy safe habit.

It happens that this no longer makes sense. Almost all running gear is led, often through a lead block only a couple of feet away, to a winch on to which it is wound tangentially in a series of clockwise turns. When the line is cast off, the turns are stripped axially, leaving a residual twist in the rope which forms kinks. When the fall is coiled it has to be given a twist in the direction of coiling in order to make the turns lie flat and when the line runs out from the coil this twist

(*Opposite*) How a kink forms: (1) turns wound on to a winch barrel; (2) accumulated twist as the turns are stripped; (3) the twisted rope kinks in the adjacent sheave

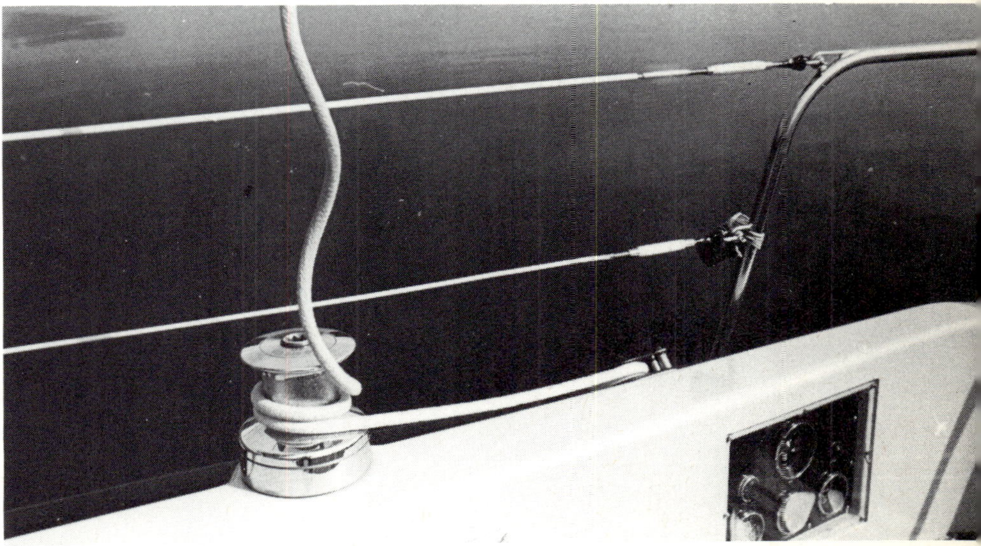

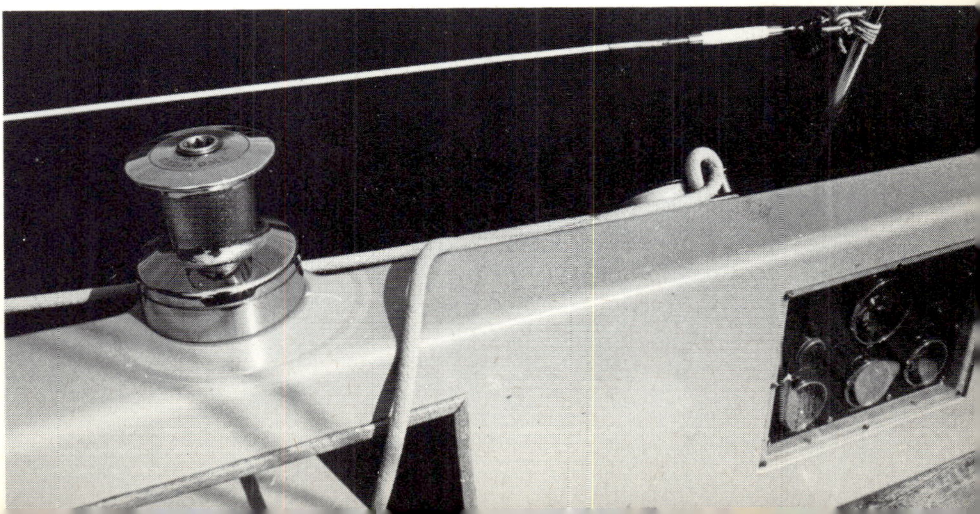

remains in it. The only way to remove the accumulated twist is to unwind the coil by rotating it, and for this reason a coil of wire rope, which is ruined if allowed to kink, is uncoiled from a turntable. A line coiled clockwise accumulates twist in the same direction as it does when turned round a normal winch barrel and thus makes even more kinks when it is cast off and allowed to run out.

As rope is so pliant, accumulated twist is not particularly obvious to the eye, though it is there all the same, waiting to fill the line with kinks and sabotage your efforts. Hosepipe, however, is wayward intractable stuff that refuses to behave unless it is treated exactly right so I have used it for the illustrations and recommend that you experiment with it.

The neutral coil: If you try to coil a line without introducing twist, the turns will form figures of eight. The resulting coil is neutral; it can be pulled out straight without accumulated twist, but it is bulky, unstable, unsightly and easily becomes disorganised and snarled. Regularly reversing the direction of the turns in a flat coil is even more impractical, but a flat coil can be made with all turns running the same way and without accumulated twist if round turns are alternated with half hitches. I know this sounds ridiculous. The very idea of putting half hitches in a coil seems lunatic but in practice it works better than a conventional coil. If made with equal care, the neutral coil is more stable, its turns do not so easily become interwoven, and, since it straightens out without kinking, the line can be pulled out horizontally from a coil lying on the deck with less likelihood of the underlying turns being tripped. It can also be made clockwise or anti-clockwise, regardless of the type of rope construction, and as will appear later there are advantages in coiling anti-clockwise. Its one disadvantage is that it takes a little longer.

(*Opposite*) What happens when a conventional coil is straightened out:
(1) the turns lie flat because a continuous twist has been introduced in coiling;
(2) this twist remains in the line when it is straightened and . .
(3) forms kinks

As it is slightly easier for someone who is normally right-handed to make the neutral coil in an anti-clockwise direction this is the method I shall describe.

1 Hold the standing part of the line in the left hand with the part to be coiled pointing towards you.
2 With the right hand palm downwards and bent down as far as it will go, and the rope running through it, reach out and grasp the rope at a distance suited to the size of the coil.
3 Bring the right hand upwards to the left, raising the knuckles to bend the hand up as far as possible and pass a round turn to the left hand.
4 Keeping the knuckles raised and swinging the arm up, reach out again for a similar amount of rope.
5 Bring it down into the left hand, at the same time bending the right knuckles downwards. At the end of this movement the newly formed turn will be lying across the back of the right hand, forming a half hitch.
6 Transfer this from the right hand to the left.
7 Repeat from 1, adding alternate round turns and half hitches. Notice that the wrist position at the end of each movement is the same as at the beginning of the next and if the arm is allowed to relax the wrist movement induces a flowing alternately over-and-under motion which soon becomes a knack.

The neutral coil can be made either clockwise or anti-clockwise but if made anti-clockwise it may be started by a series of round turns equal in number to the turns on the winch, thus eliminating all

(*Opposite*) Straightening out a neutral coil: (1) the alternate round turns and half hitches have equal and opposite twist which cancels out;
(2) the last half hitch is passing its twist on to cancel that of the final round turn by capsizing the bight between them and
(3) leaves the line perfectly straight—compare with (3) in the previous series of photographs

Making a neutral coil, counterclockwise version: (1) this man has the standing part of the line in his left hand, with the part to be coiled leading towards him. His right hand grasps the length for the first round turn with wrist bent fully down;

(2) passing the first round turn into the left hand. The movement of the right wrist imparts the twist needed to make the turn lie flat;

(3) starting the half hitch. The right wrist retains the backward bend it had in (2);

(4) a strong wrist movement with arm relaxed throws a half hitch over the right hand. The fingers of the left hand are here gathering it in while the final position of the right wrist is the same as in (1) which is the next movement

Turns on a winch barrel neutralised by an equal number of counterclockwise turns in the belay

sources of kinks. Alternatively the turns on the winch can be neutralised by the introduction of equal number of left-handed round turns in the belay, which can be done conveniently in the case of sheets but is not always possible with halyards, unless they are of wire and can be turned round cleat and winch together without being cumbersome.

Provided that the line is free of turns to start with, it is not necessary to begin coiling at the fixed end and proceed towards the free end as is essential with the conventional method. The neutral coil can be made in a line whose ends are both made fast and so, when used for halyard falls that interesting hazard of losing a halyard aloft is eliminated, because the bitter end can be made fast permanently at the dead length needed to secure the working end when the sail is unbent.

Secutity and stowage: The whole purpose of coiling a line is to organise it for instant use. The operation is a waste of effort if the coil is allowed to become disorganised by careless handling or insecure stowage. It might just as well be dumped into a bag because it will all need to be sorted out again before the line is fit for use. The practice of jambing the falls of halyards behind their standing parts is just about tolerable for short lengths and inland waters, but at sea a much more reliable means of securing them is needed if they are to be kept fit for action and prevented from washing overboard.

The easiest way of securing a halyard fall is to twist up a bight close to the cleat, pass it through the coil and loop it over the upper horn of the cleat. The advantages of this method are extreme simplicity and the fact that it is foolproof, it being impossible to cast off the belay until the coil is completely free. It does not, however, hold the coil very securely and except in quiet weather the fall needs regular attention.

A more secure but emphatically not foolproof method is to form a larger bight with a single half turn in it and pass it twice through the coil. A detailed description accompanies the illustrations. A little practice is needed in judging the size of bight needed, because the

Two ways of securing coiled halyard falls: (1) simple and foolproof but not very secure; (2) secure but not foolproof

coil must be held snugly up to the cleat and not allowed to dangle but, properly done, this type of seagasket keeps a coil fit for use for several days. It is, however, vital that everyone on board understands and practises the method because there are two possibilities to be guarded against when casting off.

1 It is possible to cast off the belay as soon as the coil has been lifted from the cleat and without the turns of the bight having been properly cleared. The coiled fall then ascends the mast intact.
2 Passing the turns of the bight the wrong way round the coil in an attempt to clear them generates an instant rope puzzle far beyond the capacity of anyone stupid enough to do this.

The first of these possibilities is symptomatic of a lack of understanding of the purpose of the coil. It is perpetrated by people who unthinkingly dump the coil on deck anyhow, not by those who have learned to lay it down carefully, right side up. The second is extremely difficult to achieve if the original job was properly done, but nature often compensates the conspicuously obtuse by endowing them with a devilish cunning, and I have seen it happen twice.

When spare lines, warps and so on are stowed away they need making up so that they are still in good order when they are retrieved. There are various methods of doing this, using a part of the line itself. Some are more effective than others but, if used, a single method should be adopted as standard practice for the ship so that someone breaking out a line that another has stowed, perhaps in the dark, knows what to expect. If several different methods are used, confusion and waste of vital time can occur when a line is urgently needed. Alternatively, coils can be stopped with short lengths of small stuff, at least two to every coil and more for big ones. The result is more secure, is instantly intelligible to everyone, and in an emergency the stops can be cut. A long warp preserves its organisation and often stows more easily if it is coiled really big, generously provided with tight stoppings, and then twisted into a sausage.

Making the sea gasket shown in previous photograph: (1) reach through the coil and grasp the standing part midway between coil and cleat;

(2) introduce a half turn in the bight by turning the hand over and then draw it through the coil;

(3) pass it over the top and

(4) back through the coil again, encircling only the turns of the coil;

(5) pass a second turn round the top of the coil in the same way, changing hands if necessary to facilitate the subsequent reversal of the coil;

(6) the two turns of the bight completed. (The bight has been exaggerated here for clarity: it should barely protrude through the coil which is then reversed and hung on the cleat as originally shown in the second picture of securing a coiled halyard)

10
Traffic

10

Other ships rank second only to fog among the hazards that threaten the small-boat sailor and even fog owes most of its menace to the risk of collision.

The classic advice to 'see and be seen' is a good starting point. Without vigilant lookout, the impending collision cannot be detected in time for it to be avoided, and unless you are seen by the other fellow in sufficient time he can do nothing about you. Good lookout depends primarily on a proper appreciation of its necessity, on alertness and the use of a systematic technique. It can be fostered by example. If skippers and watch leaders show interest in ships at a distance, other members of the crew will take to reporting them at greater ranges. Special attention may have to be given to the blind areas which some boats have, typically on the lee bow and the weather beam, either by stationing lookouts to cover these areas, as is necessary when other craft are at close quarters, or by the helmsman yawing a few degrees from time to time so that the blind arc does not permanently cover the same segment of the horizon. Bad weather, rain, spray and strong winds reduce visibility and inhibit lookout by causing the crew to cower in protective postures, and it can be quite a test of self-discipline to maintain a proper watch when sheets of icy spray are driving across the deck. In these conditions, if the strength of the crew allows, lookouts should be detailed individually and relieved at frequent intervals, then one man knows that for the time being it is his responsibility and that he will not have to endure it for too long. Systematic scanning is essential: if the lookout does not scan the whole horizon through 360° a ship will sooner or later arrive suddenly at close range, as if from the bottom of the sea.

To make a yacht conspicuous and so improve her chances of being seen is a matter of contrast rather than colour, and of sails rather than hull, because the sails are bigger in area and their predominantly vertical lines are more obvious at sea than horizontal ones. An all-white sail plan is conspicuous only under a very limited range of lighting conditions; in poor visibility or poor light, white sails can become almost invisible. Dark sails on the other hand always show up well and if there is some white in the sail plan the contrast makes it stand out even better, especially if the division of colour is vertical. Stripes have a less dramatic effect at a distance than at close range because when looking at narrow stripes the eye tends to blend the colours so that the striking contrast of blue and yellow appears green, just as the narrow red and white stripes of 'Old Glory' look pink.

Making a boat visible to radar is an interesting exercise in priorities because until someone succeeds in producing that marvellous dielectric onion, the Luneberg lens, in a form whose weight and price are compatible with small yachts, we are left with the unwieldy corner reflector and the problem of where to put it. The requirements that have to be met if a reflector is to work satisfactorily are:

1 It must retain its correct shape. A corner reflector's performance depends upon its plates being flat and accurately angled to one another, so it must be mounted in such a way that it is not subjected to accidental knocks or to loads capable of distorting it.
2 It must maintain the right attitude. The correct 'catch-rain' attitude for octahedral reflectors should now be well known, though some are still to be seen mounted with their points vertical, which makes them virtually useless except when the boat is sailing on her ear. A means of compensating for angle of heel is desirable.
3 It must be sited high enough for it to be 'seen' at a useful range and to make it distinguishable above the returns from a rough sea. In practical terms this means as high as possible and not lower than 5 metres above water level. In theory, too great a height can give rise to sporadic fading but in the context of normal yacht dimensions this is not serious enough to offset the practical advantages of height.

4 It must be free from interference and shielding. Interference is caused when reflections from a nearby object, such as a metal mast, are received by the radar out of phase with returns from the reflector and so weaken or cancel them. Shielding is the masking of the reflector by a radar-opaque material such as sea water soaked into sails.

So where are we going to mount the radar reflector? Assuming you are prepared to accept the weight and windage and give it precedence over other things you want to put there, the masthead might seem to be the best place because it is the highest point and the problems of interference and shielding are therefore avoided. But when it comes to securing such an aerodynamic grotesque so that it can neither deform nor come adrift it appears that unless it is designed to be rigidly mounted it will be hard to avoid the additional weight, complication and cost of a purpose-designed bracket or even a frame. So the masthead is an unlikely site, except in a biggish boat with more than one mast, and most of us sling the thing up in the rigging with lanyards which are light and renewable and can be adjusted to restrain excessive movement without imposing loads that would distort.

At night a vessel's lights often make her more conspicuous than she would be by day under similar weather conditions but distance is difficult to judge and even after long practice you can be badly mistaken. White lights are more misleading than coloured because a dim white light close at hand is indistinguishable from a bright one further away, while red or green lights present a clearer impression of relative brightness and distance. A major problem is posed by the unlit yacht whose crew shine a torch on her sails when you approach in the mistaken belief that this will make clear what she is and where she is going. All you see is a dim, wavering apparition with no recognisable shape, which gives not a clue to the direction of heading or point of sailing, and which a non-sailing man would be hard put to it to recognise as a sail at all. As often as not the light is switched off after a few seconds, leaving you wondering whether the crew of the other boat have really seen you or whether they were just having a look at their sails. Of course no one ought to go around without proper navigation lights, but if for some reason they cannot be used, the right course of action for the darkened vessel is to keep out of everyone's way and have ready a white light that can be shown as soon as she doubts her ability to keep clear by her own efforts. If this white light is a flashlamp it should be directed not on the sails but full at the oncoming vessel where it will be interpreted as a single white light to be avoided.

The modern masthead tricolour light is perhaps the most valuable improvement to have been made in existing yacht equipment this century. Optically efficient, electrically economical, it enables a yacht to be seen clearly at a useful range, regardless of sea state or sail trim. As a precaution against bulb failure and to enable correct lights to be shown when under power, pulpit and stern lights are needed and these should be displayed when underway in harbour, in preference to the masthead tricolour, because at close quarters they give a more intelligible picture of the boat and her movements.

However much trouble we take to make ourselves conspicuous, and however vigilant our own lookout, there is unhappily no certain way of knowing that the other ship has seen us, apart from entering into an exchange of signals. Even if she alters course in apparent compliance with a rule enjoining her to keep clear, she may be doing it for a reason unconnected with us, and we must continue to treat her presence as a hazard until she begins to increase the range. In narrow channels the situation is straightforward; small craft behave like pedestrians, keeping out of the roadway and crossing only when the road is clear; our safety is in the shallow water where the big chaps can't get at us and don't have to worry about us. But in the open sea the problem becomes complicated by the rule which says that in most circumstances a power-driven vessel must keep out of the way of one under sail. Some have said that it would simplify matters and we should all know better where we stand if the rule

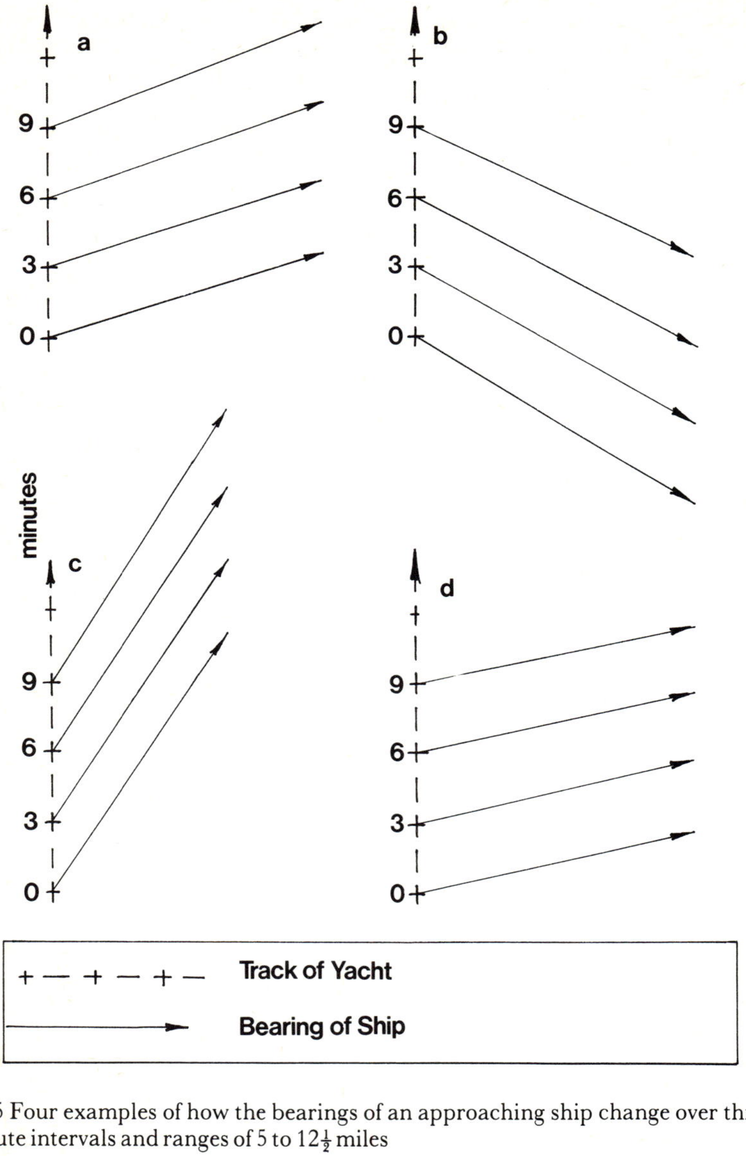

Fig 5 Four examples of how the bearings of an approaching ship change over three-minute intervals and ranges of 5 to 12½ miles

Fig 6 (*Opposite*) The situations behind the diagrams in Fig 5, correspondingly lettered

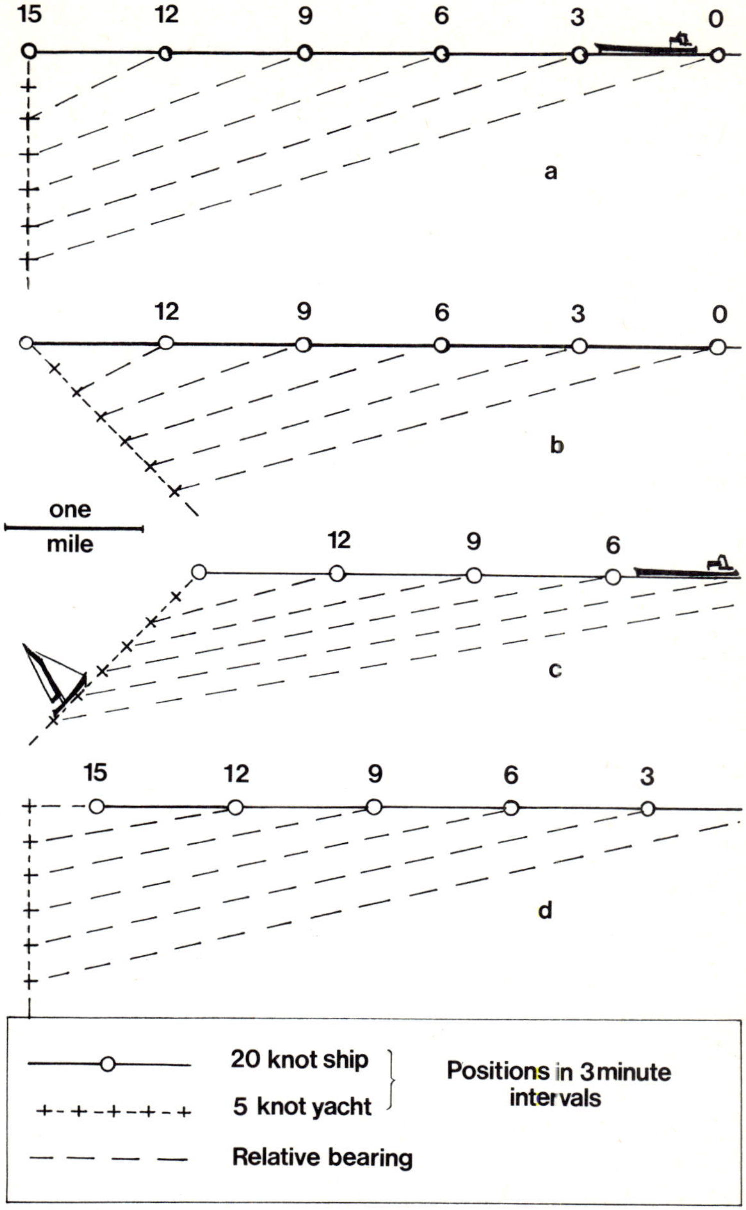
15
12
9
6
3
0
a
12
9
6
3
0
b
one
mile
12
9
6
c
15
12
9
6
3
d
20 knot ship
5 knot yacht
Positions in 3 minute intervals
Relative bearing

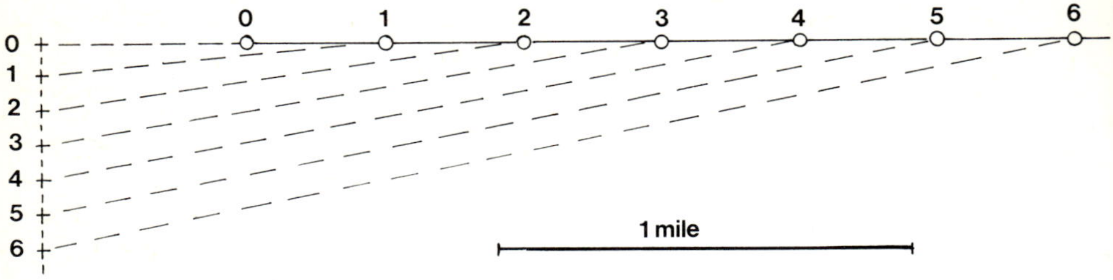

Fig 7 Anxious countdown: an enlargement of the final six minutes in *d* in Fig 6, showing the positions and relative bearings of the two vessels at intervals of one minute. Although the yacht crosses half a mile ahead of the ship the outcome would not be clear to her crew until the last moments, and they might well decide to turn back

were to be reversed, but the original rule was made inevitable by our dependence on the wind, which makes compliance with the alternative uncertain. In the open sea we cannot dodge into a shoal. Even if there happens to be one handy, it is the last place we want to be when there is any sea running, so we must meet large fast ships in the common fairway where we quickly learn that standing upon our rights is a sure course for an anxious and probably short life.

The International Regulations for Preventing Collision at Sea oblige the stand-on vessel to keep her course and speed; they *allow* her to take action 'to avoid collision by her manoeuvre alone, as soon as it becomes apparent to her that the vessel required to keep out of the way is not taking appropriate action' and they *require* her, 'when collision cannot be avoided by the action of the give way vessel alone, to take such action as will best aid to avoid collision'. The question we have to decide is, how long do we wait for the other vessel to take action before deciding that she is not going to do so?

Let us imagine four situations in which a yacht doing 5 knots under sail sights a ship on a crossing course at about 5 miles range and starts taking bearings of her at three-minute intervals. Her navigator plots these bearings as shown in Fig 5 over a period of nine minutes by which time the range has closed to one and a half or two miles. What conclusions can he draw from the exercise and what might he be thinking of doing about it? The only information available to him are these bearings, which he will scarcely ever be able to measure with this precision, and a visual estimate of the range. When you have perused this question turn to Fig 6 which shows the relative positions and bearings up to the points at which the tracks of ship and yacht intersect.

The ship which is travelling at 20 knots crosses ahead of *a, b* and *c* by an adequate $\frac{1}{4}$ mile margin and is a mile away by the time the yacht crosses her wake. In each case, the rate of change of bearing is less than 5° per minute until the vessels have closed to $1\frac{1}{2}$ miles. The yacht in *d*, on the other hand, crosses a $\frac{1}{2}$ mile ahead of the ship and, although the miss distance is doubled, the bearing is changing so slowly that her people must be in serious doubt as to whether they are going to make it until the final moments. In this case the rate of change of bearing remains less than 5° per minute only six cables separate the two vessels. The final six minutes of the encounter in *d* are enlarged in the next diagram, which shows the relative positions and bearings at intervals of one minute.

These diagrams show that it is futile to try to judge merely by eye whether the bearing is constant or changing and also that it is essential to start taking bearings early in the encounter so as to offset the low rate of change by using as long a time span as possible. They also enable us to see that the same situation can appear differently to the man on the ship's bridge from the way it does to the crew of the yacht. On the relatively stable bridge the officer of the watch, able to measure bearings to the nearest degree, may be reassured by a small but progressive change of bearing several minutes before the yacht's crew, who will be doing well if they can achieve an accuracy of plus or minus 5°, can tell what is happening. This may explain why yachtsmen often feel that big ships plough on in apparent indifference to their presence. Sometimes they do and unhappily the small, slow, vulnerable yacht has no means of knowing whether the ship has seen her and decided that there is no need to take any action or whether

her presence is undetected, unless the ship makes her intentions clear by altering course. It is this uncertainty about what is going on behind those blank pilot-house windows that makes most of us avoid situations like *d* that give us right of way over a much faster vessel. However we are sooner or later bound to find ourselves in this position through the presence of other traffic, poor visibility or plain error of judgement and then we need to have an escape route clearly in mind so that we can get out of trouble without having to wait while we think what to do.

The yacht's safety lies in her handiness. Provided that she is not hampered by a spinnaker or other impediments to quick manoeuvre she can alter course almost instantaneously on to any heading on which she can sail and as quickly turn again if the need arises. The most direct escape route out of a suspected collision situation is to turn the shortest way on to a course at right angles away from the projected course of the other vessel. When the turn is an equal 180° either way, she should turn in the direction that will most quickly present her stern to the ship. Unless the decision to turn has been unduly delayed, a fact which can easily not be realised until the turn is in progress, it will probably not be necessary to turn all the way on to the perpendicular course; it may for instance suffice to straighten up on a heading parallel to the ship until it is safe to cross astern of her. It is, however, vitally important to watch the ship closely throughout, so that instant response can be made to any action she may take. In theory there is a risk that turning towards the other vessel may produce a dangerous head-on situation, and the rules prohibit a power-driven, stand-on vessel from turning to port for a vessel on her port side, but this risk is greatly reduced when there is marked inequality in the two vessels' turning capability. Provided that the yacht is alert to detect and respond to a turn by the other vessel, she can be on a new heading before the ship can stop her initial turn.

Meeting a single ship is a relatively straightforward business, compared with negotiating a concentration of traffic and in poor visibility a small vessel should if possible avoid areas of dense traffic. An increasing number of such areas are being designated as Traffic Separation Schemes in which a pattern of one-way traffic is mandatory, and which no small vessel should approach without having thoroughly digested Rule 10 of the International Regulations for Preventing Collision at Sea.

A basic requirement of our ability to comply with Rule 10 is an accurate knowledge of position on approach to the area. This should not present any problem when proceeding to seaward or in areas like the Straits of Dover where there are plenty of navigation marks, but anyone making a landfall on the Bishop Rock or the Lizard would have to be able to get an accurate fix at least 15 miles off, which is obviously not always possible, and the lanes north-westward of Ushant now extend to 35 miles from the island. Passage planning needs to include careful consideration of the tactics to be adopted in avoiding or negotiating areas where there are separation schemes, and must anticipate the effects of a change of weather. Bad weather will often face one with the decision whether to round a headland in the inshore traffic zone or to stay outside the area altogether, and only a sound understanding of the behaviour of sea, wind and weather can enable a correct decision to be made.

Crossing of traffic separation schemes is sometimes unavoidable and, though beset with regulations, it does have the advantage that, rogues apart, you only have to cope with traffic coming from one direction in each lane. The rules say that you must cross at right angles to the direction of traffic flow, but where tidal streams are strong they will cause a discrepancy between the yacht's course and her track over the ground so that her movements do not appear the same to a shore based observer as they do to another ship, and the navigator needs to be perfectly clear about his intentions. The purpose of crossing at right angles is to reduce the time spent in the lane to the minimum possible and to present a clear-cut encounter situation to ships using the lane. Both these aims are achieved by steering a *course* at right angles to the lane axis: steering *to make good a track* at right angles to the lane axis results in the crossing taking longer and in the yacht appearing to other ships to be crossing obliquely. If a yacht steers the correct course she will of necessity be set down by the tide and a shore-based radar will, like her own navigational plot, show her to be crossing diagonally. The discrepancy between course and track becomes marked when the tidal stream is parallel to the lane and exceeds half the yacht's speed, which it may easily do in some areas.

11
Compass Error

11

The compass does not often feature as a source of navigational problems or as a major element in marine suspense dramas, but over the years a fairly steady stream of incidents involving unexpected deviations and other reputedly aberrant behaviour has appeared in logs of cruises or been recounted over consoling pints. The manner in which these incidents have been described and the measures taken in the course of averting their consequences frequently reveal an underlying suspicion that the compass in question has developed some inexplicable fault. This attitude is by no means confined to the inexperienced. Even seasoned voyagers have let slip remarks that betray some uncertainty about what they really expect the compass to do.

The sailors of the twelfth century were fairly uncritical of 'the needle'. When clouds obscured their primary directional references in the sky, they went through the quasi-magical ritual of touching and floating the needle and it seemed to them that it pointed unfailingly to the pole star. But when later the needle was carefully balanced and mounted on a pivot in the protecting *bitacle* to form the earliest proper compass they began to notice a discrepancy and blamed it on the makers, whom they accused of faulty workmanship. To keep them quiet, some of the instrument makers took to offsetting the magnet on the card so as to make it read true north and, as long as these supposedly 'corrected' but actually confused compasses did not go too far from the workshop in which they had been made, the mariner was satisfied. The great ocean voyages which were made in the fifteenth and sixteenth centuries, however, brought more evidence and fresh conclusions had to be drawn.

By the time that the idea of a mysterious affinity which attracted the needle to the star had been replaced by a theory of magnetism which recognised that the magnetic pole was displaced from the true celestial pole, the pilots concluded from very meagre evidence that on a certain meridian in mid-Atlantic the compass did indeed point true north and that the 'error' increased with departure to the east and west of this meridian. This proposition was also doomed to be demolished by experience, but already a habit of mind had been formed, the expectation that demands the creation of myths had been established and the misunderstanding of men fathered a fictitious 'error' on the instrument that had exposed their own inadequacy.

The so-called 'error of the compass' is defined as the algebraic sum of variation and deviation. Neither variation nor deviation are attributable in any way to the compass itself and the word 'error' needs to be kept firmly in quotation marks: to equate it with fault is like blaming the cop who catches you speeding. Before we decide what we can expect of a compass we need to consider the nature of the force that makes it work.

The earth's magnetic field seems an unlikely candidate as a reliable directional reference because it is extremely erratic. Not only has it undergone repeated reversals of polarity, but it is in a continuous state of change at a rate which is itself changing. Most of us have a mental picture of a field which corresponds with that of a huge but relatively short bar magnet buried in the centre of the earth offset from the rotational axis and radiating lines of force which emerge steeply through the surface and curve round the globe to become horizontal at the equator. But the bar is bent. Its poles are by no means 180° apart. The field between them is to say the least kinky, and the magnetic meridians do not in general point directly towards either pole. So we can expect that a compass, in the absence of other influences, will align itself with the local magnetic meridian, but not that it will point to the magnetic pole. This leads us to variation which is defined as the angle between the magnetic and true meridians at a given place and time. It is a strictly geophysical phenomenon independent of the compass so that while it can be spoken of correctly as 'magnetic variation' it is misleading to call it the 'variation of the compass' as is sometimes done.

The intensity of the earth's magnetic field is quite weak; it requires only a small magnet to overcome it locally and reverse the indication of a compass, but not everyone realises how much the directive horizontal component of the field is affected by the angle of dip. In the British Isles the field of force plunges into the ground at 70° to the horizontal so that less than half the total intensity is available as a directing force for the compass. At the magnetic equator the field is horizontal, so the whole field strength is directive, while at the magnetic poles the field is vertical and there is no directive force at all. This becomes important when we consider the field in the location of the compass itself, where the earth's field is distorted and weakened by that resulting from magnetic material in the vessel. A faultless compass aligns itself with the horizontal component of the field in which it is situated and so provides the means of measuring deviation. This is defined as the angle between the north point of the compass and the magnetic meridian: it is a manifestation of the ship's magnetism and although it forms a part of the so-called 'compass error' it should not be thought of as a defect or fault in the compass itself.

In hulls of wood, glassfibre or non-ferrous metals, deviation can be very small or even eliminated if the compass is sited away from magnetic componenets and is guarded against such random influences as tools, food and beer cans, apparatus using direct current, some photographic light meters and steel or nylon in clothing and personal gear. Steel and ferro-cement hulls need to have their magnetic fields in the vicinity of the compass neutralised in order to reduce deviation to acceptable limits. Although this process is known as compass correction, it is strictly not the compass that is corrected but the field surrounding it. If the vessel is to make voyages involving large changes in magnetic latitude it is essential that each component of her magnetic field be neutralised by an equal and opposite field *of the same kind*, otherwise the changes in the earth's directive force will not be matched in the ship's field and unexpected deviations will appear. Correction for heeling error is upset by change in magnetic latitude, which may introduce fresh deviation and a check swing ought to be done when the change of latitude has exceeded 15°, or when the vessel has crossed into the opposite magnetic hemisphere.

It is a sound and time-honoured principle that the deviation should be checked whenever the opportunity for a reliable comparison arises. This is very easily done and you soon get into the habit of looking out for a convenient transit so that you can check the deviation for the heading you are on even though, according to the deviation card, there is none. But if you do find an unsuspected deviation, try to find the cause, which is extremely unlikely to be in the compass itself.

The most likely reason for a change in deviation is that some portable magnetic material has got too close to the compass, so check the surroundings including the people, who often have surprisingly magnetic things about them. If you suspect a fixed fitting it can be checked without removing it by sliding a portable compass such as a bearing compass towards it along a non-ferrous straight edge with which the lubber line is kept parallel, when any deflection of the card will be seen. I once had to pilot another yacht whose compass went crazy after someone had whiled away a dull watch by removing all the compensating magnets and putting them back haphazardly, so it is a good idea to make a note of which magnet goes where.

It is very simple to test the serviceability of the compass itself because there is so little that can go wrong.

1 Check the security of the mounting and make sure it has not become misaligned.

2 Look for bubbles or discoloration in the liquid.

3 With the boat on a constant heading (i.e aground or secured alongside) note the heading. Deflect the card as far as possible using a small magnet which must then be moved at least 6 feet away from the compass, and watch the card carefully. It should move smoothly back to a little beyond its original mark and settle to within a degree of the same heading after one or two

further oscillations. Repeat, making the initial deflection equal but in the opposite direction.

Defects revealed under the first item can be rectified easily. The others indicate leaks, deterioration, pivot wear or loss of magnetic vigour, all of which need a professional overhaul.

Replacing a compass does not alter the causes of deviation but there is nevertheless a possibility that the new one may respond differently, so a fresh swing should always be carried out.

12
Seamanship in Harbour

12

Not many years ago there lived a man, now cut off when not much past his prime to the grief of his friends but I doubt not to his own gain, with whom I shared many an anchorage. I remember him moving about his deck in the morning twilight, a burly figure in a hairy jersey he had acquired in Iceland, rousing his crew from their bunks with his favourite cry, 'Harbour rots ships and ruins men'. To this free spirit harbour was prison, a place to escape from, and so it will be to the few stalwarts like him, now and in time to come. But for most of us harbour means security, the mind runs on to 'haven', 'breakwater', 'landlocked', 'mooring', 'Port after stormie sea'. How is it then that more accidents happen in harbour than at sea?

The actuary may point out that most private craft spend far more time in harbour than at sea, that they tend to remain in harbour during bad weather and that hardly any go to sea at all during the worst months of the year. He may also indicate that, human wickedness apart, the usual cause of damage is contact with other vessels, the land or the obstructions that are attached to it, and that in harbour these are all nearer and more abundant. If he happens to be a seaman as well he may add that crews tend to be off their guard, and to take chances that they would not consider at sea where they are reminded continually of the power of the elements.

The seaman tends to take a sympathetic view of accidents at sea, reserving censure even when he feels there has been contributory negligence. He recognises the influence of diverse and subtle pressures, and with an inward 'There but for the grace of God go I' looks for the lesson to be learned rather than the individual to be blamed. But accidents in harbour more often arouse his scorn than his sympathy because most of them are foreseeable and are brought about by want of foresight.

The factors that have to be considered in harbour, and the actions that have to be taken, depend on the reason for being there and on the circumstances that prevail.

The Transient Halt

There is sometimes a need to wait for a fair tide or a shift of wind or to pay a short visit to the shore. In settled weather an overnight anchorage would come into this category. The circumstances can vary greatly but it is normally a fair-weather exercise and even if all the crew leave the vessel they do not go beyond instant recall. The method may be to anchor with light tackle, secure to a mooring, or lie alongside. With some types of hull, beaching is possible.

The Manned Stay

The intention here is to remain in harbour for twenty-four hours or more, with the boat under the supervision of her crew, who would remain in the port area. The crew would not expect to have to put to sea because of a deterioration in weather but they might expect to have to shift berth. Similar methods would be adopted, though heavier ground tackle would be preferred and a more thorough check on the strength of mooring than visual assessment of its riding part would be needed.

The Unmanned Sojourn

When leaving a boat unattended, even though someone has undertaken to keep an eye on her, the mooring arrangements have to be able to cope with any eventuality. The boat can be moored by her own ground tackle, using at least two anchors, left on a permanent mooring by agreement with the owner, or, if there is no alternative, berthed alongside. In some places it will be possible to choose for oneself the method of bringing up, in some the anchorage may be entirely filled with moorings and in others it may be compulsory to lie end-on between an anchor or mooring and the shore. In this last case the considerations are a combination of those relating to anchoring and mooring alongside.

Planning

All Harbours Regardless of Method

1 *Degree of shelter*: Will the harbour afford protection throughout the period of stay? If not it will affect your whole approach to the problem. For instance, if a shift of wind will by itself oblige you to leave you cannot regard your stay as other than a transient halt; you must be ready to leave at all times and there is no point in using other than light ground tackle. If the harbour is sheltered, except in strong winds from a limited sector, it is suitable for a manned stay but not an unattended sojourn.

The havens on frequented coasts are usually very fully described in sailing directions written specially for yachts and published either commercially or by clubs, but once you get off the beaten track you must choose your anchorages from the chart and the Admiralty Pilot, and to many people this is one of the most interesting aspects of cruising. Many good small-boat anchorages do not rate a mention in the Pilot, which is written with larger vessels in mind, but there is still plenty of useful information for those who are prepared to look for and interpret it. 'Affords no anchorage' saves you the effort of further investigation, while 'small vessels with local knowledge can find shelter' means that you are on to a promising trail if you take care and have a large-scale chart.

The best shelter is found close to a low-lying weather shore with trees on it, clear of any tidal stream. Increasing distance from the shore, height and bareness of the land, and strength of stream all render an anchorage less secure and, though the worst possible anchorage is in the narrows of a long fiord-like inlet among high mountains, any of these factors can by itself be critical in determining the degree of shelter, so an apparently snug little land-locked pool can be an intolerable cauldron of howling squalls if it is set in the heart of high mountains. Similarly, a tide can raise a sea and cause boats to sheer about, subjecting their ground tackle to heavy strains in an apparently well-sheltered estuary.

Evening in a well sheltered anchorage behind low ground. A warm front whose advancing cloud can be seen near the left horizon will cause the wind to back and blow from the left of the picture during the night

2 *Depth of water and nature of bottom*: Will there be enough water during your stay? Alexander the Great's fleet found themselves high and dry because they failed to appreciate that the tides in the Arabian sea were bigger than those in the Mediterranean. If anchoring for a couple of hours on a rising tide there is clearly no problem, but if the tide will fall before you leave, the depth at low water, and at subsequent low waters if the tides are making, can be important.

The nature of the bottom affects holding ground and whether you can accept grounding at low water: in a strange anchorage it is a good plan to use a lead line to sample the ground in several places round the chosen berth. Taking the ground at anchor limits the times when you can move and may expose you to danger of fouling by shallower-draught vessels when the tide turns or the wind shifts, but in deep soft mud even a deep-keeled yacht should sit comfortably upright and suffer no ill effects. If there is a risk that sea-water inlets may be buried close the seacocks beforehand. If the bottom is hard or uneven always inspect the area at low water before grounding.

3 *Traffic and anchorage pattern*: When entering a strange harbour take plenty of time to size the place up and do not be in a hurry to bring up. Notice how moorings and anchored craft are distributed and how they are lying. Yachts of deep draught lie tide-rode while shallow-draught boats and dinghies lie to the wind, so you have a visible indication of the relative strength of each. Fairways may be indicated by lanes through moored craft or by focal points for traffic such as fish quays, ferry landings and so on. If there is a clear area that looks an attractive berth in a well-populated harbour, suspect that there may be a better reason for it being empty than that no one happens to want to occupy it. It could be empty because it needs to be kept clear for moving traffic, because it is the regular berth of the pilot boat or the harbourmaster's launch, or because of an underwater obstruction.

Yachts often crowd together round the anchoring mark suggested by the local pilot book or close to the most convenient landing place. This often amounts to choosing a short row in the dinghy at the cost of a disturbed night when most people, if they thought about it, would sooner have peace and quiet even if it means a longer row.

Methods of Bringing-up

Anchoring with a Single Anchor

Anchoring is the easiest way to bring up and is the most comfortable, peaceful and private way to lie. The strength and condition of your own ground tackle are known factors and the boat is free to adjust her position by swinging. On the other hand getting underway involves rather more physical effort and is more complicated than leaving a swinging mooring. It may be ruled out if the water is excessively deep, if the bottom is unsuitable, so obstructed by moorings or otherwise fouled that there is no room to anchor.

1 *Principle*: An anchor is a device able to dig in to the sea bed and take a hold when a horizontal strain is put upon it, but which can be levered out by a vertical pull. All anchors except pure weights must move *some* distance horizontally while they are taking hold. An anchor may fail mechanically if subjected to a heavy enough load, but the holding power of an anchor of any strength is limited by that of the ground in which it is buried. Eric Hiscock has quoted 30 lb as the minimum weight at which any type of anchor can be relied on to get a proper grip. I endorse this view and further add that although certain anchors of advanced design and great holding power are capable of digging in at lighter weights than this, the ground itself may break up because the smaller anchor is incapable of getting hold of enough of it. This can result in the anchor dragging through quite viscous mud, or uprooting and dragging a lump of really stiff clay in which it remains embedded and is thus prevented from getting a fresh hold. When anchoring with a chain cable the minimum ratio of scope to depth at high water is usually given as three to one, but this figure needs some interpretation, since what matters is the weight of chain hanging in catenary, which both ensures a horizontal pull to the anchor and acts as a spring to cushion snubbing loads. You would get away with 60 metres of cable in a depth of 20 metres but it would be unwise to rely on 12 metres in a depth of 4.

2 *Practice*: If the anchor is to bite properly and quickly, the chain must follow it to the bottom without any check until at least twice and preferably three times the depth have run out, and it must not land in a heap on top of the anchor but pay out along the bottom so that the anchor starts to dig in as soon as the cable is snubbed. To achieve this involves preparation. Check that anchor and cable are cleared away and ready to run, making sure that nothing has been put in the cable locker on top of the chain and that the chain itself has not been disturbed as can easily happen in rough weather. I once found a whole cable weighing 150 kg had been flipped and inverted during a rough passage so that the bitter end was on top and we had to overhaul the entire length before the anchor could be let go. If the

cable cannot be relied upon to pay out from the locker, it will be necessary to range the required amount on deck.

The superior strength and durability of synthetic fibres has led to an increased use of rope cables, or warps, especially in the United States, where the sound of a chain cable running out is said to signal the arrival of a British yacht. A warp's lightness allows great lengths to be carried and lightens the work when weighing, both great advantages when using deep anchorages, though by the same token greater scope must be used. Its disadvantages are the bigger swinging circle required; its vulnerability to chafe, which can be only partly offset by interposing a few fathoms of chain between it and the anchor; the comparative difficulty of cleaning and stowing it compared with chain; and if the boat is of the light-displacement, short-finned type that tends to sheer about, the warp can immobilise and endanger her by becoming woven around her underwater projections. The warp's convenience for temporary anchorage is undoubted, as is the security of chain in the long term, but it seems to me that the greatest benefit of warp is that it allows a shorter total length of chain to be carried than would formerly have been thought necessary. Instead of carrying the maximum length of chain you are ever likely to require—say 80 metres—you can carry the greatest length you commonly use, which would be more like half this amount, and add nylon to its inboard end on the occasions when you need more.

3 *Judging where to drop*: The textbook method is to mark the anchoring spot on the chart and identify it by cross bearings (transits if possible) on prominent features, but you may find when you arrive that you cannot anchor in this position because the berth is obstructed, or you may see a better spot. What you have to do is visualise the swinging circle, whose radius is your boat's length plus the eventual scope, with your anchoring point at the centre, and then place that circle so that it is clear of all obstructions. If there are other boats you will need to try and visualise their swinging circles. Not easy but you can make an intelligent guess if there is enough wind for them to be putting some strain on their cables. If they are lying head to wind you

Fig 8a The only promising space in a crowded anchorage. Wind and tide are together and it is not difficult to estimate the positions of these boats' anchors and their swinging circles

Fig 8b Swinging circles of the boats in Fig 8*a*, in solid line. Pecked lines define the areas (radius = combined boats' lengths) in which anchoring is certain to cause fouling of the boat or her ground tackle already there. The best place for the newcomer's anchor is on the line joining the sterns of *C* and *D*: if she anchors in the middle of the visible space she will foul *B*. If all the boats were of similar type none would foul any other, but the high-sided shoal draft motor boat and the full-bodied gaff cutter with her low freeboard and rig are unlikely to swing parallel with the others

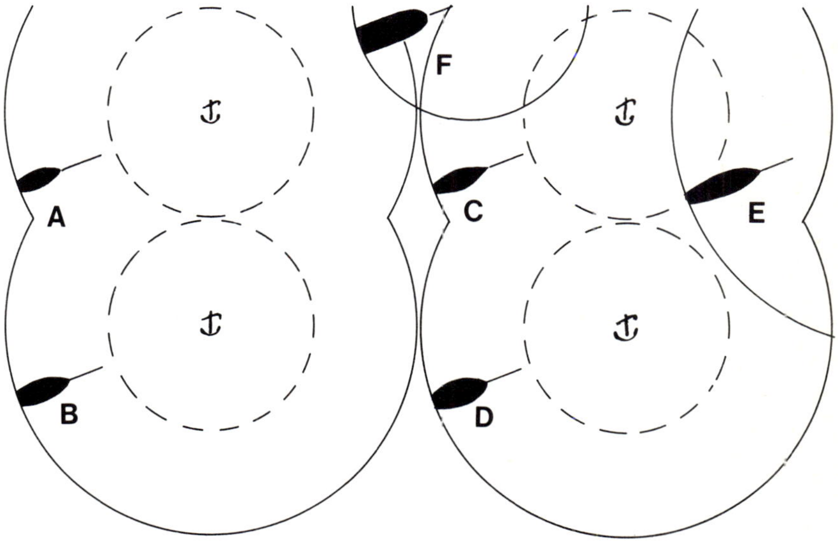

Fig 8c and d The same situation but with wind against tide. All the sailing boats are lying to the tide but only *D* is fully tide rode: the rest are being driven past their anchors by the wind. *F* is completely wind rode and would be a menace to *A* and *C* were she anchored rather than on the shorter scope of a mooring. *D* could remove anxiety about fouling *C* and *E* by putting out a kedge on her port bow. The newcomer now finds it more difficult to judge where to drop since all the boats have moved closer to their anchors and sterns no longer give any clues to swinging circles. She needs time to observe the others' movements and should drop midway between *A*, *B* and *C*. She will have to lower her mainsail before anchoring

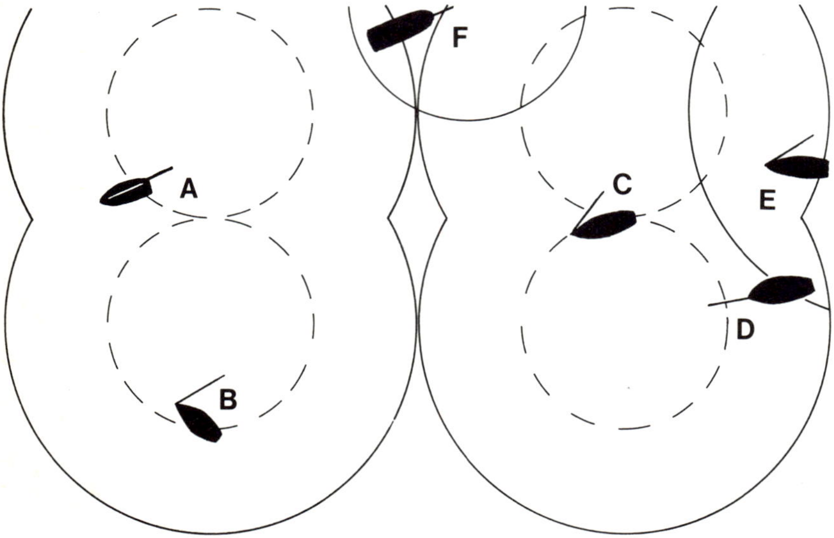

can locate their anchors roughly from the depth of water and probable scope of their cables or warps. If you drop on or outside the periphery, your swinging circles will intersect but you will not foul another boat of similar general type if the wind shifts, and neither you nor she will find one of you lying over the other's anchor when the time comes to get underway. The easiest position to judge is to note a boat that is anchored outside anyone else's swinging circle and let go close to her stern. When wind and tide are in opposition, boats normally lie closer to their anchors, whose position may be difficult to estimate, so you must imagine a circle round each boat and drop outside that. Remember that a shift of wind or turning tide will make you almost certain to foul a boat or her ground tackle if you drop within your two boats' combined lengths of her anchor, even if you manage to lie initially clear by veering more cable.

Boats on moorings usually have less scope and therefore a smaller swinging circle than anchored boats, so you must allow for the difference when anchoring near one and anticipate the effect of a shift of wind that would put you in the weather berth. When a mooring is unoccupied the buoy may give no clue to its real position and you can easily find that you have foul-berthed a mooring that seemed well clear until the owner returns and hauls in the slack. If this happens it is good manners and good seamanship to shift your berth, although even the rightful owner of a mooring is not entitled to secure to it if this results in his giving a foul berth to a boat that was previously anchored there.

Anchoring is just about the most leisurely operation known to seamen and unnecessary hurry is one of the commonest reasons for doing it badly. When done properly, way is taken off the boat in the position in which she is to be anchored and then as she drifts away under the influence of wind or tide the anchor let go. In a breeze and the absence of tide the boat can be luffed head to wind, the sails lowered as she shoots into position and then, when she has lost way, she pays off and begins to drift. This is the point at which the anchor is let go and the required amount of cable paid out while she drifts broadside on to the wind. The cable is then snubbed and, held by the bow, she swings head to wind confirming that the anchor is holding. If she remains broadside on it indicates that the anchor is dragging. In a light air, when the drift alone would not be enough to lay out the cable and dig in the anchor, the boat can be given a sheer and the anchor be let go while she still has steerage way. When coming to an anchor under power in a calm and no tidal stream, the berth is approached either towards the direction from which wind is expected, or the most exposed quarter, way is taken off and the boat allowed to gather slow sternway before the anchor is let go. Snubbing the cable, when moving stern first like this, loads the tackle much more abruptly than when drifting broadside on and care is needed to see that sternway is not excessive. In order to check that the anchor continues to hold, line up convenient marks on the land or take bearings.

Mooring with Two or More Anchors

A single anchor may not suffice for a number of reasons:

1 Lack of space making it necessary to reduce the swinging circle.
2 Tides in the anchorage which would cause the boat to range about and perhaps trip her anchor.
3 Poor holding ground, limited shelter or deterioration of weather requiring greater holding power.
4 The boat has to be left unattended.
5 The boat has to be secured precisely in a certain position. Though not an unimaginable requirement, this is unusual and would be met by a tight four-point mooring.

In cases 1 and 2 it is usually best to arrange the two anchors in opposite directions, up and down stream in a tideway, middling the boat between them with taut cables, seizing the cables together and then veering more cable until the junction is well below the keel. A strong blow at right angles to the line of the anchors could put an unacceptably heavy strain on the ground tackle, so if this is likely more scope should be allowed between the anchors so that the angle between the cables when both are under strain is less than 60°.

The circumstances in which a second anchor is most needed are when the first proves to be inadequate on its own, has been lost or has had to be slipped. Thus the second anchor needs to be no less powerful than the first, and the widespread practice of carrying a light-weight kedge as a second anchor is irrational. A boat should have two bower anchors of similar holding power though they might be of different design. Up to about 10 tons TM they can be of equal weight, but in bigger boats the 'spare' could well be rather larger than the anchor in regular use.

For what I have called the transient halt, a light-weight, easily recovered anchor is a great convenience, but if you think of it by its apt American name, 'lunch hook', you will get it in true perspective as a third anchor and not try to use it as a second bower or for kedging yourself off the mud. As it can be below the 30 lb minimum weight it should be of efficient design and as light as possible for ease of handling and stowage.

Laying out an Anchor by Dinghy

The need for two anchors is sometimes not apparent at the time when you bring up. In theory it would seem easy enough to veer some cable and manoeuvre the boat into position for letting go the second anchor, but in practice it usually turns out to be simpler to lay it out using a dinghy. This is one of those exercises that is simplicity itself if done right, but if done wrong can be a back-breaking and even dangerous struggle, with a strong chance that at best the anchor will go down in the wrong place. It all depends on having a clear idea of what you are going to do and on careful preparation. The aim must be to take the anchor to its intended position, paying out the warp as you go, drop the anchor cleanly and then set it home by taking a strain on the warp. The actions are:

1 Bend the warp on to the anchor.

2 Load the anchor into the dinghy. If the dinghy is pneumatic and has a suitably shaped stern it may be possible to lay the anchor across the buoyancy tube in such a way that it can be launched by the tightening of the warp or a push of your foot. If the dinghy is rigid or of unsuitable shape it is best to suspend the anchor below the stern with a light slip-line that is secured by a quick-release knot. Only if the anchor is light enough to lift with one hand and launch without rising from your seat should it be carried inside the dinghy.

3 Flake at least as much of the warp into the dinghy as will suffice to reach the dropping point, beginning with the part next to the anchor. If the warp is of laid rope and fairly heavy (16mm or more) it can be coiled, though many experienced seamen frown on the practice: the coil must be carefully made turn by turn into the bottom of the boat and not put in already coiled. A single check to the free running of the warp can ruin the operation.

4 Check that the warp leads clear from the dinghy in through a suitable fairlead and make fast the bitter end on the parent vessel.

5 Station a hand to tend the warp on the parent vessel's deck.

6 Row out to the dropping point, paying out warp as you go. If there is a tidal stream it will carry the warp away downstream as you pay it out so head upstream first as far as is necessary and then work into position across the tide.

7 On reaching the dropping point check that all the warp is out and release the anchor. If there is still warp in the boat go on, if there is room, until all has paid out before dropping. If you cannot go on because of shoal water or the risk of fouling other ground tackle, get your partner to haul in the slack from his end.

8 While you return to the boat, have your man haul in the slack steadily until he gets a good strain on the warp and then belay it. This will settle the anchor into the ground and when you get back aboard you can complete the adjustments and rig the chafing gear.

Recovering the Anchor

A shift of wind or deterioration of weather can make it necessary to shift berth or even clear out of an anchorage under adverse conditions when a strong wind or rising sea can subject the ground tackle to heavy loads or violent snatching. Such conditions demonstrate the fallacy of using the weight of the ground tackle as the criterion of the effort required to raise it.

If a competition were held to determine who could exert the greatest sustained pull on an anchor cable while standing on a typical foredeck, the difference between the winner and the worst performer might look quite impressive when compared with the weight of a thirty-footer's anchor, but when compared with the strains that the same thirty-footer is capable of imposing on her ground tackle in heavy weather they are insignificant.

The problem is most acute in the smaller boats. Not only are boats above a certain size normally fitted with adequate windlasses but there is enough room for several people to work together on the foredeck. In small boats it can be a problem for even two people to find the necessary space to exert themselves efficiently. The difficulty, however, is not so much gaining anything on the cable as hanging on to what you have recovered. If anchored with a warp, this is comparatively easy, provided you have strong enough winches, because even if the mooring bollard or cleat is too awkwardly placed to allow you to catch a quick turn you can lead the warp aft to a mast or cockpit winch. For a chain cable the most useful device is the simple but rarely seen chain pawl which can be mounted in the bow fairlead but must be strong.

The technique of sailing out the anchor, by which the boat makes a series of short boards up to her anchor, putting herself about by the strain on her cable as it grows out toward the beam, is the best to use in a strong wind but needs a smart hand on the foredeck, able to snatch a turn when the strain starts to come on, and to haul in smartly whenever the cable goes slack. A chain pawl is particularly useful in this operation.

Motoring up to the anchor in heavy weather is more difficult because if you use enough power to retain full directional control you overrun the anchor, and if you do not the bow tends to pay off in the gusts. Once again you have to be able to hang on to what you have gained until you have swung back head to wind.

Dragging

When a boat is properly secured by her ground tackle in a blow she lies uneasily, ranging about, yawing and heeling and making a good deal of noise and fuss. You can recognise all her movements while lying in your bunk in the dark. The gusts shake her, throwing her bow round and pushing her to leeward. She heels and sags, straining at her cable and raising a great length of it clear out of the water, increasing its pull on her bow until she can move no further and swings abruptly into wind, coming upright and surging forward as she does so. As the gust eases, the weight of her cable sinking back on to the bottom draws her ahead, waves slapping against her bow, until equilibrium is restored or the next gust repeats the cycle. As long as this goes on you can relax and drowse as best you may among the commotion, but if she lies quietly, adding no voice of her own to the wind's uproar, and heels steadily to one side you must turn out and assert yourself for she is going absent without leave.

Inadequate scope, denying the anchor a truly horizontal pull, is the most common cause of dragging and it is better to err on the generous side than to incur all the consequences of being mean with the cable. If swinging room restricts scope, compensate by suspending a weight on the cable. Dragging can also occur if the anchor is prevented from getting a hold by such things as rubbish or weed on the sea bed or by ground that is too hard. If the initial hold is in kelp or rock an increased load may cause it to break with treacherous suddenness. It can drag through weak material like volcanic ash or soft mud. It can be tripped by becoming fouled by a bight of the yacht's own cable or a change in the direction of pull. Setting the anchor in the way already described ensures that it gets an initial grip. Checking the holding ground in unfamiliar anchorages by consulting the Pilot, using the lead, or seeking local advice help to avoid unreliable ground, but patches of kept or rock can lurk in good anchorages.

The vulnerability of the fisherman-type anchor to fouling and tripping is well known and it is an imprudent man who lies to a single fisherman for more than a few hours or in an anchorage subject to tidal streams. But patent anchors can also break out when the direction of pull changes, and although they are supposed to dig in again they do not always do so. I have on rare occasions had CQRs up to 60 lb hold through hours of gale only to break out upon a major shift of wind. I suspect that although a CQR tends to draw itself into an upright position as it buries, it may in stiff ground obtain a powerful hold while still on one side and depending on the accident of its attitude relative to the ensuing shift, it may either bite deeper or break out complete with an encrustment of clay which prevents it from getting a further hold. The trouble has seemed entirely random, occurring in the same places and under the identical conditions as have before and since failed to cause it. The answer is either to lay out a second anchor in the direction of the expected shift or be standing by in your oilskins when the shift comes.

A Foul Anchor

Sooner or later there comes to everyone the day when, with crew booted and spurred, sails hoisted and a tide to catch, the anchor cable comes bar-taut straight up and down and comes no more. The frustrating but unfailingly interesting saga of another fouled anchor begins to unfold.

There is no certain way to avoid this predicament, but you can go a long way towards it. You naturally avoid anchoring where diamond-shaped beacons indicate the shoreward ends of submarine cables, or where these or abandoned cables are marked on the chart. You consult the Pilot to see if any mention is made of foul ground, wrecks, lost moorings or ancient ferry chains. You suspect places that have seen better days—former fishing harbours, commercial ports, the environs of industry or the armed forces, anywhere in short where anyone might have had the opportunity (not reason mark you, the merest possibility is enough) to deposit anything big enough to embed itself immovably into the mud. You avoid anchoring in such places if you can, and if you cannot you use a tripping line.

As its name suggests, a tripping line is a device to pull an anchor out in the reverse direction to the way it went in. It consists of a length of stout line, one end of which is made fast to the crown of the anchor and the other to a buoy. The line must be strong enough to stand up to a powerful pull from a windlass, long enough to reach the surface at all states of the tide, with up to 100 per cent extra if the stream is strong. It must not be buoyant or it may ensnare someone's propeller. The buoy should be big enough to be obvious to passing craft and marked to indicate that it is not a mooring buoy: if you are tempted to use a couple of net floats because you have not room to stow a proper buoy use a large fender instead. When bringing up, the buoy is streamed and the line paid out before letting go the anchor. The line ought not to be stopped to the cable or brought back aboard the yacht because of the risk of it getting turns round the cable or fouling and tripping the anchor.

On shortening in the cable, it becomes possible to recover the buoy with a boathook and the slack can be gathered in, taking care not to trip the anchor prematurely. If the anchor is found to be foul, slacking the cable and hauling in on the line should clear it. If the fluke is tightly wedged this may need a powerful pull. When the anchor refuses to budge and you have not rigged a tripping line, everyone will inundate you with ingenious suggestions. Try the simplest measures first. Do not assume that the anchor cannot be broken out and brought to the surface until you have proved it. Use the boat's buoyancy. Assemble all the crew as far forward as they can get, heave the cable as tight as can be, make fast and then have everyone hang outboard over the stern for a few minutes before going forward again, when you may find there is some slack. On a rising tide you may need only to wait patiently.

If this fails, keep the strain on the cable and motor about in different directions, then slacken off the cable and repeat several times with increasing amounts of scope each time. If the anchor comes free of the bottom but still seems to be foul, try to winch it up to the surface, then hang the foreign body off on a slip-line while you get the anchor clear and out of the way. Extricating the anchor from whatever is entangling it may involve working from the dinghy with a risk of becoming trapped and injured or even dragged to the bottom if anything carries away, so it is vital that the object is well secured.

Continued failure may at least yield some clues about what has happened and so suggest further lines of action, but for want of any specific indications I would next aim to get a line on to the crown of the anchor and try to recover it from the opposite direction to that in which the boat is lying. The first step would be to lay out a kedge, equipped with a tripping line and buoy, as far as possible upwind and use this to haul the yacht's stern into wind while keeping the fouled anchor's cable taut up and down, so as to raise the shank of the anchor as nearly as possible in line with the cable. The next move is to pass a bight of chain, wire, or failing either, weighted line down the cable and try to 'feel' it past the shackle and as far along the shank as possible. When it is believed that the bight is clear of the cable and round the anchor, several fathoms of cable can be paid out on the spot and then, while continuing to pay out cable liberally and checking out the bight so that no strain comes on either, the yacht is hauled astern by her kedge warp as far as can be done without risk of starting the kedge. Gently taking a strain on the bight and progressively increasing it should work it up to the crown of the anchor which can then be expected to follow.

Lying to a Swinging Mooring

This is the most convenient method of bringing up, provided that you are sure of the strength of the mooring and that it will not be required during your stay. It is negligent to leave the boat unmanned until you are satisfied on both counts.

Inspection of the visible parts of a mooring may be enough to tell you that it is not strong enough for your boat, but in order to confirm that it is strong enough you must either go diving or find someone who knows, and anyone who knows this much will probably be able to say whether anyone else will require it during your stay.

Moorings get in a mess if they are left unused and it is difficult to conceive of any owner objecting to someone lying to his mooring, provided that he can get back on it himself when he needs it and find it undamaged. But, if it is irksome to come home and find your mooring occupied by an uninhabited boat, it is also bewildering and frustrating to find a strange harbour so congested with moorings that there is nowhere to anchor and the vacant buoys devoid of any clue as to the size of their parent boats or when they will be needed again. So if you own a mooring you can help yourself and others by marking the buoy clearly with your boat's name and tonnage, and attaching a small waterproof label (one of those toy dinghy fenders or even a plastic bottle serves admirably) giving your date of return, such as 'Back Sunday p.m.' or 'Back 25 Aug.' The chap who picks it up will not only bless you and be disposed to treat your tackle carefully but with luck he may be inspired to mark his own mooring when he gets home. Even the churlish 'KEEP OFF' is better than a blank buoy.

Swinging moorings consist of a ground chain with one or more anchors, and a riding part, to which the vessel secures and which is connected to the ground chain by a swivel. From the user's point of view, moorings fall into two categories, depending on how the riding arrangements are rigged, which is usually dependent on local conditions.

1 *The permanent buoy*; In this system a large buoy supports the riding chain and the user secures either to the buoy itself or to a pendant which may be of synthetic rope, wire rope or chain, attached to the riding chain and possibly equipped with a small pick-up buoy. The advantage of this system is that it is easy to use and if used regularly stays clean. The disadvantages are that, unless the water is heavily polluted, weed and mussels accumulate on the upper part of the

riding chain, on the buoy and, if the mooring is left unused, on the pendant; also the pendant sometimes gets snarled up so that even if you can get hold of it you cannot bring it aboard. As excessive wear can occur if the buoy becomes unloaded in use, it is usual to arrange for the connection between the pendant and the riding chain to pass through the buoy itself, and if the shape of the buoy is such that the upper eye can come into contact with your hull it may be necessary to heave it up close to the stem in order to avoid damage to topsides.

Steel buoys are still to be found here and there. Avoid them like the plague for, though they may be strong enough to hold you ten times over, they can sink you. If there is either wind or tide but not both it is just possible to lie to such a buoy, using a long scope of warp, but if there is any stream you will be continually having to fend off and in rough weather you will have a hard job to stop it smashing you up. Increasing the scope to try to get clear can result in your becoming dangerously and inextricably entangled.

2 *The pick-up buoy*: If the mooring is fairly light it is sometimes preferable to let the riding chain lie on the sea bed when it is not in use and recover it by means of a stray line attached to a light pick-up buoy. The advantages of this system are that the chain does not get fouled by marine growth when it is lying on the bottom and the boat's way is checked more gradually when bringing up to the mooring. The disadvantages are that if the water is deep it can be hard work hauling the riding chain to the surface; in some anchorages the buoy rope may become very dirty and the chain may bring mud on deck; the buoy rope may be cut if overrun by a large power-driven vessel, parted by a clumsy attempt to bring up, or damaged by the ignorant or careless, who may make fast to it instead of to the riding pendant. This type of mooring has much to recommend it in unfrequented anchorages and clean water. In deep water the weight can be reduced by substituting nylon for all but the bottom of the riding scope. The buoy rope should be strong.

When lying to any mooring, especially when the boat is to be left unattended, make sure that fairleads and mooring cleats or bollards

An anchor warp demonstrates its need for protection against chafe (*John Watney*)

Anti-chafe gear on a mooring pendant; fairlead closed by a pin; message buoy with date of return

and their fastenings are strong enough and that you eliminate chafe. Neglect of these points is probably the prime cause of most damage. A warp under strain quickly chafes through and a derelict drifting through a crowded harbour can cause widespread damage just because no one took five minutes to protect her warps with a parcelling of stout canvas or a length of heavy hosepipe, or to ensure that she could not pitch her cable out of its fairlead.

Berthing Alongside

For a transient halt this is often the most convenient way of bringing-up, especially if the reason is to visit the shore. For longer stays it is usually more troublesome and attended by greater disadvantages and risks than any other method and should only be used for an unattended sojourn if no alternative exists. The sole advantage of berthing alongside is that it facilitates the transfer of people and materials between the vessel and shore, consequently it is ideally suited to embarking and disembarking crew, the loading or unloading of stores and equipment and to effecting repairs involving heavy tools or shoreside services such as mains electric power. The disadvantages are that intruders have unobstructed access; your boat becomes a fender, a pontoon and a thoroughfare for anyone berthing outside you; dirt comes aboard on the wind and on people's feet; since the boat cannot swing it is often a problem to get enough ventilation without letting in rain or dust; you lose all privacy, and though you and your marine neighbours may have the consideration and good humour to rise above this among yourselves, it is mortifying to think that if you were to stare into the homes of the sightseers on the shore as they are staring into yours they would send for the police. Even in remote and uninhabited places there is great risk of damage when lying alongside, unless the berth is a really sheltered one like a canal basin. If there is a fetch of even a couple of hundred yards, you will need to take special precautions against the chafing of warps and the displacement of fenders, and even then it is safer to clear out and anchor off.

The best alongside berth for a manned stay is outside another vessel that will still be there when you leave—a laid-up fishing boat, for example. When you have come alongside, secure temporarily, make sure that your fenders are doing their job, that neither of you will take the ground and heel over at low water, and set about getting properly moored. Unless the other boat is so much bigger than you that you cannot get your lines past her, you should rig bow and stern lines to the shore, forward and after breast ropes and springs to the other vessel. The length of bow and stern lines will have to take account of the tidal range and, if sharing bollards on the quay, the eyes of your warps should be passed from below upwards through the eyes already there before being dropped over the bollard. In this way any line can be cast off without interfering with any other. Before finally settling your lines to the other vessel, check that your rigs cannot collide if set rolling by the wash of a passing vessel.

For a prolonged stay or if caught alongside in heavy weather and unable to clear out you must take all the precautions against chafe mentioned earlier and also protect ropes where they lie over the edge of the quay. The best method here is to use lengths of chain from the shore and bend warps on to them clear of the masonry. Chafing gear will be needed on your mooring lines where they pass through fairleads or come into contact with other vessels. The light pneumatic fenders normally carried in yachts should not be used, unless the boat is manned, because any sea will cause them to climb out of position. They should be replaced by heavy ones or, best of all, old tyres which will stay put even if they do make dirty marks on topsides.

For small craft, berthing alongside in heavy weather is only safe in really sheltered situations. If a sea gets up big enough to cause the boat to pitch or roll appreciably she is in danger of serious damage and should be moved on to a swinging mooring or her own ground tackle.

Berthing end-on

Common in the Mediterranean, berthing end-on between an anchor and the shore is economical of space because yachts can be packed gunwale to gunwale; it avoids the need for crews to cross other boats' decks when going ashore, and getting under way and bringing up causes less disturbance to one's neighbours than when lying in tiers alongside. It is useful wherever shelter is complete but swinging room restricted. It suffers most of the disadvantages of berthing alongside, and berthing and unberthing can be tricky if the wind is strong. I suspect that the custom of lying stern-to became established because the overhang of a standing bowsprit and its rigging ruled out the alternative, but unless the boat has a long bowsprit it is preferable to berth bows on. This can usually be accomplished simply by dropping an anchor from aft on a warp which is then paid out as the yacht is taken into the berth, when a bow line can be passed ashore. Going ahead, she is under much better control than going astern.

Lying bows on, results in less dust and shore dirt coming below, renders your domestic life invisible to the public ashore and if you or anyone else makes a mistake and causes a collision with the shore it is your strong bow that takes the knock, almost certainly above water, and not your deep stern with its vulnerable appendages, a point to bear in mind in places liable to seiches. When the shore consists of natural rock this may be the only way to lie if you aim to be able to reach the shore without recourse to the dinghy.

If it is essential to berth stern-to, the lack of precise control exhibited by most auxiliary yachts when going astern under power makes it necessary to run a line ashore with the dinghy while lying to the anchor, and then haul the stern in while veering cable. Only when the wind is blowing straight in to the berth will it be possible to do otherwise, as in this case the yacht will line up with the berth and can be checked in by veering the anchor cable.

Last Word

We began with the proposition that seamanship is the ability to achieve our objectives on the sea by recognising and exploiting favourable conditions and exercising proper management, and, just as the development of this theme has been coloured by my feeling that our natural interest in, and mental affinity for, the material is well enough developed to need no further urging, so I have seen no need to devote a separate chapter to the fashionable subject of safety.

Accidents cause suffering, waste and inefficiency and we have good reason to seek every means to reduce them, but the pursuit of safety as an end in itself seems to me to be as unrealistic and unproductive as the pursuit of happiness, for both are the by-products of other aims. The successful achievement of objectives at sea, or anywhere else, presupposes the matching of competence to aims and results in our being as safe as we have any right to expect in an existence in which the ingredient of danger is, from the moment of conception, as constant and perhaps as necessary as oxygen.

The link between safety and happiness will not be lost upon the followers of any sport that combines hardship and privation with an element of risk. Neither is accessible without confidence, and confidence comes from understanding so thoroughly what you are doing that you are at ease and in your element. Our mythical pioneer on his raft found his confidence wavering when the storm came down on him off the headland, but, thanks to his sense of priorities, he was able to turn the experience to good account. It is thus that confidence grows.

Acknowledgements

The coastal views at the chapter openings are by Captain the Honourable F.C.P. Vereker RN who drew many of these views between 1883 and 1897. They are produced through the courtesy of the Hydrographic Department, Ministry of Defence and by permission of the Controller, HM Stationery Office. Most of the views are very wide and with the exception of Lundy Island only sections are shown as follows: 1 Set and Drift, Old Harry Rock; 2 Berry Head open of Downend Point; 3 Lundy Island; 4 Start Point light house; 5 Longships light house; 6 Gosport, Trinity Church open west of Spit Fort; 7 Dartmouth Harbour entrance; 8 South Foreland light house, arrows indicate south face of Shakespeare Cliff in line with Lord Warden Hotel; 9 Bishop Rock light house; 10 entrance to Crookhaven; 11 Mewstone; 12 Lough Carlingford, Haulbowline Rocks light house; Index, Black Head, St Austell Bay.

Index

Index